AF574772

FLAT JACK

FLAT JACK

THE AUTOBIOGRAPHY OF JACK SIMMONS

JACK SIMMONS
WITH BRIAN BEARSHAW

Macdonald
Queen Anne Press

A Queen Anne Press BOOK

First published in 1986 by Queen Anne Press,
a division of Macdonald & Co (Publishers) Ltd
Greater London House, Hampstead Road, London NW1 7QX
A BPCC plc Company

British Library Cataloguing in Publication Data

Simmons, Jack, 1941–
Flat Jack.
1. Simmons, Jack, 1941– 2. Cricket players–
England-Biography
I. Title II. Bearshaw, Brian
796.35′8′0924 GV915.S5/

ISBN 0-356-10969-0

Typeset by Sunrise Setting
Reproduced, printed and bound in Great Britain by
Hazell Watson & Viney Limited,
Member of the BPCC Group,
Aylesbury, Bucks

For Mum, Jacqueline and Kelly

CONTENTS

1
THE GOOD LIFE

I still can't believe it's all true. It's just like a fairy tale. When I was twenty-six I was a draughtsman in Preston and a Saturday afternoon professional in the Ribblesdale League. And that, I thought was to be my life. I didn't expect anything else. Then right out of the blue Lancashire asked me to sign and now here I am, nearly twenty years on, still a Lancashire player, with nine Cup Finals to look back on, a record six-figure benefit, ten years in Tasmania, and one of *Wisden*'s Cricketers of the Year. True, I haven't played Test cricket, but I reckon I have had a lot more out of cricket than lots of Test players I know. And I hope there's still more to come.

There's not much disappointment in getting a £128,000 benefit, but one after-effect I didn't like was when people asked me why I was still playing. Why does a man, who is turned forty, with £128,000-plus in the bank, continue playing? It disappoints me that people can even ask that. I still play because I enjoy it and when the time comes when I don't, then I'll know it's time to give up. And as long as Lancashire want me to play, that's good enough for me.

Cricket has given me a hell of a good life. Everything we've got has come through cricket. I know people said to me after the benefit: "Well, you won't need to go to all those functions now, presenting trophies and prizes, speaking all over the place." But that's the way I am. We have money in the bank now, we are right for life, we have a nice house, two cars, we lead a good life, and everything really, when you boil it down, has come through cricket. My wife, Jacqueline, worked all her life until 1981, so naturally she has contributed a lot to our success. In the benefit year she would be going to quite a lot of functions and getting up at half past seven to go to work. Yes, we would have been comfortable, both of us working and me being a pro on Saturday afternoons. But now it's completely different. We can go anywhere in the world we want and not bother. And we must never forget that it is all down to cricket, and the people who support it.

People say to me: "If you had gone to Lancashire when you first got the chance, at eighteen or nineteen rather than when you were twenty-seven, do you think you would have played for England?" I don't know. Tell you what though. I am a gambler but I wouldn't change it. Not a minute of it. Not for anything. Jack Bond, who was my captain in my first five years at Old Trafford, was right when he said I could have been on the staff for three years and then been sacked and never thought of again. But I arrived when one-day cricket arrived, which was good for me. It helped me get used to the high standard of first-class cricket. The John Player League really brought one-day cricket home to the public, perhaps even more than the Gillette Cup had done. There was a game on television every week, people could see a complete match on Sunday afternoons, and its fast pace really suited the casual supporter. And it was the sort of cricket I had been playing for years, right up my street. It was easier to catch the eye, with smaller performances, twenty odd runs and three wickets, and you had done a good job, perhaps even won the game. So confidence was built up and spread into the first-class game and for me that was an ideal introduction.

Of course I am bound to wonder what might have happened if I had joined Lancashire when I was first asked at the age of nineteen. I had been for trials, played with the second team, and Stan Worthington, the old Derbyshire and England player, was coach when Lancashire first asked me to join them. At the time, it was more important to me, and in particular my mother, to complete my apprenticeship as a draughtsman, to give me a real base for the future. After all, I was the first member of our family to really have a trade. I was told Lancashire would come again when my apprenticeship was completed but they did not arrive, so off I went into league cricket as a professional. Looking back now, I can remember how excited I felt when Blackpool, one of the top League teams in the north, asked me to be their professional in 1968. That was the peak of my career then, and to see my name on the wall alongside such great players as Hanif Mohammad, Bill Alley, Cammie Smith and Rohan Kanhai as the Blackpool professional was an enormous thrill. I was frightened, too, having to follow players of that quality but luckily for me, I think I had three hundreds and a ninety in the first few innings. It was because of that early-season form that I was chosen to play for the Northern League against the Ribblesdale League at Blackpool.

By this time everything had changed at Old Trafford: a new secretary, a new coach, even the committee had been voted out since the time I had been asked to join the club. The coach now was Buddy Oldfield, a former Lancashire and Northamptonshire batsman who had played for England and who lived on the Fylde Coast near Blackpool. Maybe that was one reason he went along to watch the league representative match where he had heard that there were a couple of youngsters in the game worth watching. I did pretty well in that game and three or four days later, there, on the doormat, was an envelope containing Lancashire headed notepaper asking me if I was available to play in a second-team match. Well, I'd have walked down to Old Trafford. I would have crawled there. I think I was on the phone to say I would play while I was still halfway through reading the letter. So a series of second team matches followed, although obviously they didn't want to waste too much time looking at a twenty-seven year-old who had been around a while. In fact, in one game, against the Lancashire League, I hadn't batted or bowled in the first innings and a message came down from the committee room to the captain, Keith Goodwin, to say: "Do you think we've brought him down here just to see whether he can field. He has to bat at number three and he has to bowl."

I was still on trial when I made my first-team debut against Northamptonshire at Blackpool. I have never been so nervous in my life, making my debut on my home ground in front of five or six thousand people. When I was taking guard my knees were knocking and needless to say I did nothing as a batsman, getting one run in the first innings and, as they say, not doing quite so well in the second. But I did bowl as well and got some nice, if unexpected, encouragement from the umpire, Cec Pepper, who had spent a lot of years in the league. I really was nervous because I knew if I performed with any measure of success I would be offered a contract for the following season. I bowled about seven or eight overs before our captain, Jack Bond, took me off. I hadn't got a wicket and Cec, again trying to make me feel better, said: "He's dropped a clanger, Jack. I thought you were just starting to get a bit of rhythm, you'd have got these two out." I said there was no way I could tell the captain in my first game that he'd dropped a clanger, so off I went down to third man. Three-quarters of an hour later I was asked to bowl again and fortunately for me at Cec's end. As I gave him my sweater he turned to me and said: "I told you I was right. They've tried three other bowlers and nobody's got a wicket and if he'd kept you on, you'd have got one out." So being really naive, I said to him: "Well, what do you think I should do, Cec?" He turned away from the batsman and said: "Jack, to the left-hander bowl round the wicket and to this fellow at this end, bowl over the wicket." So we moved the sightscreens and I bowled to Hylton Ackerman. He had a careful look at this newcomer bowling again, gently pushed four balls back, but with the fifth I rapped him on the pads. I turned round and said: "How's that, Cec?" And he said: "I told you I was right, Jack. That's out," and raised his finger. And that's how I got my first first-class wicket.

Sure enough, right after that game Jack Wood, Lancashire's secretary, said they would like me to sign for next year. Even then I wasn't certain because it was the same year Ray Illingworth left Yorkshire and there was a lot of talk about him joining Lancashire. I said it would be useless if I went to Old Trafford if Illingworth was there — I might as well stay in the leagues and keep going as a draughtsman. But Jack Wood said no, they wanted us both, and Illingworth would be playing plenty of Test matches. As it turned out, he went to Leicestershire and after Lancashire had been annihilated in only their second John Player League match I came into the team and stayed there. That year Lancashire won the new Sunday competition. And I always say that when I went there in 1969 we started to win things. I never tell anybody that Clive Lloyd went there at the same time.

For almost a decade from 1969 I seemed to be on a high with two John Player League and four Gillette Cup wins with Lancashire, not to mention the real delight of captaining Tasmania to a Gillette Cup final win over Western Australia, and leading them in their first season in the Sheffield Shield. I think if you were to put me in a corner and ask which game had given me most pleasure it would have to be that Gillette win in Australia — the first real step to getting into the Sheffield Shield on a full-time basis. Didn't I cry after that game. I'd never known anything like it. Of course, I've had disappointments, too. Like every other cricketer in the country, I would dearly have liked to have played for England. I felt once or twice I might just have crept into a one-day squad, but it was not to be. I would like, too, to have captained Lancashire. I would have considered that a great honour and again, I have got close with many years of vice-captaincy. When I returned from Tasmania one year, I was asked if I liked being captain and I said I liked the responsibility since it brought the best out of me. As far as Tasmania was concerned I knew, without being big-headed, that I had more experience than any of the players and so got their respect. But here could be a different kettle of fish because they were all professionals at Lancashire. I thought I might have got the opportunity of the captaincy when Frank Hayes and John Abrahams were appointed but on both occasions I was passed over. Still, like I tell them all: "You'll always get everything I've got, no matter who goes out there. If a dog goes out as captain, I'll always go out behind it."

2
A MEMBER AT THREE

My grandfather was regarded as one of the most promising young players ever produced by Enfield, the Lancashire League Club near Accrington. In fact, they reckon that if he had not set his mind on being a regular soldier he would have become a Lancashire player and perhaps even played for England. My father also played for Enfield and was part of the championship team of 1943. So when I was born in Clayton-le-Moors, the village that contains Enfield Cricket Club, it was only natural that I should be practising at the ground as soon as I was old enough to hold a bat. Today I still hold a playing member's card for Enfield and in 1987 the Simmons family will have completed 100 years with the club.

When my grandfather was a lad it was the practice for a player to bat at the nets until he was out. He once batted for three weeks — fifteen nights at two and a half hours a night — before they got rid of him! The only thing it brought him was a ticking off from my grandmother, who I never knew, because his tea was spoiled. After three weeks I suppose it must have been something of a mess! My grandfather lived with us for over twenty years before he died in his eighties and he and my father were a great encouragement to me to play the game.

My father used to work down "Dicky Pit," the local colliery, where he was a fireman. He then became a caretaker at Mount Pleasant Council School. Grandfather was an outstanding batsman but dad was a medium-paced swing bowler, not much of a batsman I don't think. I know if I didn't score a run, my father would say to me when I got home: "Another duck?" And my mother would say: "No matter how many he gets he'll never get as many as you." So I assumed he couldn't bat. As well as playing for Enfield my father also played for the education authority on Wednesdays and I can remember seeing him take nine wickets, catching the other, then hitting the winning runs when they were in trouble. He had a good temperament and was very easy going, quietly spoken.

Enfield Cricket Club was a way of life for us. Even my sisters, Vera and Betty, were keen on the game and they would take me to the ground in the pram and push me around. It was very much a social occasion where you saw old friends. I was born on 28 March, 1941 and was made a member at the club when three years old. The first I remember of really learning about the game was when I was about eight, when Clyde Walcott, the great West Indian cricketer, was the club professional. In those days the first team practised on one side of the ground and everybody else on the other, so I would just watch and field and bat when I could. At the bottom of our street was a meat company run by Mister Slinger who would pay for his three sons (one of them, Eddie, is now a member of the Lancashire committee) to have private tuition from Clyde who invited me along as well. I told him I didn't think my mother and father would be able to pay and he said: "There won't need to be any money from your family, Jack." Clyde was a big influence on me and in many ways became a member of our family while he was with Enfield. It was open house at the Simmons home and he would come for meals or go to Auntie Bertha's chip shop just round the corner from the ground in Whalley Road to sample fish and chips in a bag. And that's where I got a liking and a good grounding for fish and chips. Open house was even more open at Whitsuntide, especially on Whit Monday when the church Whit walks were being held. Everybody knew the Simmonses and people would say: "Come on, Ada'll have a nice cup of tea and something to eat." Mother was a very good cook. That was the atmosphere that Clyde Walcott walked into and which made him such a part of the family scene.

We didn't have a lot of money and our parents sacrificed a lot for us. I know they wouldn't let me play, no matter where, without being properly dressed and my mother would always make me clean my boots on Friday night before a game. The only thing I didn't have was a bat but Clyde gave me my first. When he went home he would write to me and I still have a letter sent to me from Perth when he went with the West Indies team to play Australia. I was only ten and the letter was addressed to Master Jackie Simmons, 12 Duke Street, Clayton-le-Moors, and written just before Christmas in 1951:

> Hello Jackie,
> I had promised to write you a few weeks ago but could never get around to it. I have not been doing so well in Australia, but to be honest I am having really bad luck. I was run out today in the match against Western Australia, it was certainly a pity as I started so well. I am probably keeping all my runs for next summer, I hope so at any rate. You must be wondering if I am keeping that left elbow straight and playing with a straight bat. I hear the weather has not been too kind in Clayton, but hope we will have a dry summer next year. Everton Weekes is still suffering from a pulled muscle and Frank Worrell is terribly out of form, which makes a great difference to our team. How is the bat going? Most of our chaps are using my bats but not getting many runs unfortunately. Say hello to your Mummy and Daddy and say I am enjoying my stay in Australia. Tell Tommy I will have to take some lessons when I return as I am doing everything wrong. I am very sleepy at the moment so I will sign off by wishing you a Happy Xmas and a prosperous New Year.
>
> Cheerio, Clyde.

I played cricket with Mount Pleasant School under-11 team and by the time I was eleven I was in the Enfield under-18 team, mainly as a batsman though I bowled a bit as well. I made my debut in the club's third team where I got a wicket with my first ball, against Accrington third team. We used to have an old player who would spend a couple of hours with the third team at practice and he would put a threepenny bit or a sixpence on the stumps. If the bowler knocked it off he got it, if you defended your stumps well enough and it stayed on, you got to take it. I'll tell you, it didn't half make bowlers keen and you'd get seventeen year-olds bowling to eleven year-olds on indifferent net wickets and making life hard. But with perhaps a tanner at stake, I was determined to stay. Jack Addison, a much bigger boy than me, hit me three times in three balls, one on each ear and one over my eye. I threw my bat down, I was so browned off with it, but still went back to make sure I got my tanner. There was never any sympathy when I got home. My father would say: "Didn't you have your bat in your hands when you got hit?" And that was it. I scored for the second team at the time, thinking I might get into the side if somebody didn't turn up and sure enough one day, when I was still only twelve, I was able to make my debut. I went in near the end of the innings, scored ten not out, and the following week I was chosen for the team. It was near the end of the 1953 season and the following year I played regularly, and by the middle of the season I was opening the batting.

I played well enough to be asked to play for Enfield's first team when I was fourteen but my father said no, he didn't think I was ready, and made one of the selectors, Eddie Talbot, promise that when I was picked for the team it would not be for just one game but for a run of three or four. Then if I didn't do anything it would be back into the second team. But at the end of that season when I was still fourteen I did make my debut in the first team. I was having a good run in the second team and was at Ramsbottom for a match when Mr Slinger drove up in his big Humber car and said: "Jack, you're playing at Burnley in the first team." I got changed in the car and I remember batting against the Burnley professional, an Australian called Wally Langdon. I went in about number seven, pushed a few back, then got a yorker that knocked all three stumps out. I had started. I was left out from time to time but I always had a chance as an all-rounder, I could always get into the side for batting or bowling. So I tell youngsters now: "You're always better off with two strings to your bow." If I had a bad run with the bat I could stop in the team because I was picking up a few wickets. I once got five "ducks" in two weeks around Whitsuntide but I was still in the side because of my bowling. I was going out to bat not knowing whether to slog or block and I just played forward, got a thick edge to third man for four, and I felt like I'd got a hundred.

It was some time before I got my first 50. In fact, I was eighteen before it arrived — 53 not out at Rawtenstall. I had been close a time or two and in one game against Nelson I was the only batsman into double figures with 40 out of 72. Johnny Wardle, the old Yorkshire and England left-arm spinner, was the professional at Nelson and he opened with seamers, then spinners, his full repertoire. He beat me time after time but I wouldn't leave my crease and when I got the chance I'd have a big whack over square leg. In the end he did get me stumped though I'd kept it in my mind all through the innings, I wanted to get 50. With such a big name as Wardle playing, the ground was packed and I'd have got a £20 collection. That grieved me, missing it.

I learned about the collections from the days of Walcott — he used to live off his collections and took my mother and father to Blackpool most Saturday nights. My father also tried to instil in me: "If you get to 40 make sure of going on to 50. You don't need to get there in two blows, ten ones will do." Very early on in my career I got to 45, then my highest score in the Lancashire League, and I got a long hop from Steve Wells, a very experienced left-arm spinner. The ball bounced halfway down the pitch, I got into it, and gave a catch. If two of you were getting near 50 together you made sure there were quite a few minutes between so there was time to get one collection properly before setting out for the second, otherwise you'd have to share one. Some players used to play for their 50s when the holidays were coming up and I know I once said when we played at Accrington that with the holidays near, a collection would be doubly welcome. I took six for 24 that day and received £4 7s 8d after Conrad Hunte, the West Indian opening batsman who was then our professional, had got £7 12s 6d for an innings of 92. Everybody got a collection for a 50 but for bowling it was six for 30 for a professional to qualify, five for 40 for an amateur, and if you looked like getting there right at the end of the game your teammates, or committee members, would wait with the buckets or trilbies and catch people as they went out. All the money was counted in the committee room and put in bags, all the ha'pennies and pennies as well as threepenny bits and tanners. I'd get on the bus home, my cricket bag weighted down with all the change — it was like carrying a ton of bricks home. Ten per cent of collections went into the players' fund for the end-of-season picnic to Blackpool. In 1959, when I was eighteen, I got about seven collections and when there was a chance of me leaving to become a professional in the Ribblesdale League people used to say I wouldn't make that much more money because I would miss the collections. Well, I'd had a good season that year, 50 wickets and 434 runs, but you can't be sure of a good season all the time.

During the years at Enfield I had also been making progress through school teams. I had failed my eleven plus exam but not by much and though I cried at the time, because I felt sorry for my mother and dad, I was happy enough to go to Accrington Technical School, which was more sports and trade orientated than a grammar school. In my second year I played cricket with Accrington Schools under-15 team, at thirteen I was in the North Lancashire team. My father was too ill to come and watch me play in one of my first matches in the team. The doctor told him the excitement wouldn't be good for him. His hobby at the time was racing pigeons and he often got me to take the birds as far as Manchester or Stoke by train and release them for practice runs. When he knew he wouldn't be able to go to Old Trafford for the game, he sent my sisters Vera, who was then aged twenty-five, and Betty with half a dozen pigeons. They had to catch two buses and a train, carrying the birds in a basket. Dad had cut out several thin strips of paper and whenever something important happened on the field involving me, Vera was to write it out, attach it to the bird's leg and release it. The birds flew home, about thirty miles, to Clayton-le-Moors, but even then Dad couldn't collect them from the pigeon loft which was about two hundred yards away. A friend of his stayed in the loft and as each pigeon returned he took the message home to Dad. "Jack has gone in to bat, just hit a four." . . . "Jack has bowled four overs, none for plenty!"

When I was fourteen I captained the North Lancashire side and I still have those funny coloured caps with Old Trafford 1954, 1955 on them. My father watched me from the ladies stand at the ground, and whatever he said, I did, and if he thought I was having a bowler on too long he would just take his handkerchief out and blow his nose. I kept hoping he didn't have a cold or I'd have been changing the bowlers every over. I remember an opening batsman from a North Lancashire v South Lancashire match called Michael Cairns, who turned up more than twenty years later when I was in the England dressing room at Melbourne Cricket Ground. He was then the general manager of the Southern Cross Hotel and later moved on to Hawaii, which is the reason I've had about five holidays there!

When I was fifteen I played for the Lancashire Federation, an under-18 team. We went on tour, stayed at the Grand Hotel in Leicester, went to Uxbridge and Hove, played half a dozen games over ten days, and it cost £8. Another game was at Worcester and during a hold-up for rain we were playing cards. I wasn't playing in the cricket match and as I've always been a gambler I was enjoying the game of cards. Right at the end we were finishing a hand just as our two batsmen went back out and the manager, Jim Gledhill, came in and went absolutely scatty. Somebody said: "We're only finishing the hand off, Mr Gledhill." He said: "That's ridiculous, your own teammates out there, and you're playing cards." Naturally, I was the youngest in the team and that night one of the older members came to me in the hotel and said: "Jack, it doesn't matter to us, it's our last year in the Federation, but you have two, maybe three years to go. Go and have a word with Mr Gledhill and apologise." So I did and explained the position, but I was never selected again. That grieved me a little bit especially when I could get 50 wickets and 434 runs against Test players, high-class players, yet I couldn't even get into the Federation side. So it taught me a lesson, although I don't think it was a fair one. Jim Gledhill has been a good friend ever since and I sometimes wonder if he remembers.

The following year, 1957, when I was sixteen, all the Lancashire League clubs were invited to send their most promising youngsters to nets at Burnley. I was there. So, too, was Peter Lever, then with Todmorden, and who was later to play for Lancashire and England, and also Stan Worthington, the Lancashire coach, who seemed more interested in me bowling leg breaks and asked if I could bowl a googly. I said I was working on it. He watched me bat and after the trials said he'd be seeing me again. When the letter came through asking me to play in the second team I felt I was brought in to see how hard professionalism was in my first game. We went to Jesmond to play Northumberland and in the team were Harry Pilling and Peter Lever, who had just joined the staff, as well as Peter Marner, Roy Tattersall, Alan Wilson, Colin Hilton, Peter Whiteley, and Malcolm Hilton, who had been twelfth man with the first team against Hampshire at Southampton. He dropped off at Old Trafford about midnight, got a taxi, boarded another train to Jesmond but arrived too late and was twelfth man for the second team as well! Wilson, the wicketkeeper, was captain and as Stan Worthington had not told him what I could do, he asked Alan Bolton, the opening batsman, about me. Bolton was having a bit of a bad run at the time and suggested I should open. The wicket was hard and fast, and looked white so Alan didn't want to go in first. But Wilson said he couldn't put me in first in that class of cricket in my first game. So he sent me in number three! I got nine and was caught by the wicketkeeper. I turned round to watch the keeper take it, then walked off with the umpire's finger raised. I was still fifteen yards from the pavilion when a shout came: "Did you hit that ball?" "Yes Mr Worthington," I replied. "Well here you bloody well walk."

I played about six games when I was seventeen and eighteen and hit a few 50s. Having a keeper of the class of Wilson helped my bowling and gave me wickets I would not have had at Enfield where the keeper, because I bowled it a bit quick, would stand two yards back. The fielding and catching were the biggest impressions I got of how big a gap existed between League cricket and even Lancashire's second team. When I went back to Enfield after playing Minor Counties cricket, although still probably the youngest in the side, I felt ten feet tall with enormous confidence to get runs and wickets.

After a few more games with Lancashire second team the following season, Stan Worthington took me on to the players' balcony at Old Trafford and said: "Son, I'd like you to go home tonight and tell your parents you've been invited to join the groundstaff at Lancashire and we'd like to know their decision." I floated home that day, like I was on a cloud, three buses and two and a half hours to go about thirty miles. Once home, we discussed it. My mother didn't want me to leave the brickyard where I was an apprentice draughtsman. I think my father did want me to go, but just said: "It's your life son, you just decide what you want to do. Go and ask Fred Wolstenholme, he'll come up with something." He didn't want to go against my mother but if I could incorporate playing and working, so much the better.

Fred was in charge of the draughtsmen and said there was no problem but he'd have to go to the three directors and ask them. I had wanted to be a mining surveyor but I didn't get the 'O' level in English that was needed and through my father's contacts, Mr John Buckley, an Enfield C.C. committee man and a manager at Accrington Brick and Tile Company, and Fred Wolstenholme, I had become an apprentice draughtsman. The directors refused to release me and said I had to choose: a cricketer or a draughtsman. So I turned Lancashire down. I think I was afraid of how long I would last. It frightened me to see the ability in the second team, never mind the first, with such players on the staff as Bob Barber, Brian Statham, Geoff Pullar, Malcolm Hilton, Alan Wharton, Ken Grieves, Tommy Greenhough, Roy Tattersall and Ken Higgs. It came home to me even more at the end of that 1960 season when seven or eight professionals were sacked or released. I had two years still to serve out my time as a draughtsman and Stan Worthington was sympathetic, though disappointed, and said: "All right, Jack, we'll wait till you're twenty-one and served your time." I had been told by Mr Wolstenholme that despite the directors' decision I would be able to play as many games as I wanted the following year, but as an amateur. After I had explained to Stan Worthington about being the only member of the family who had ever had a trade, he said he thought it wouldn't be too bad for me as there wouldn't be any problems about me losing my job if I didn't make it in cricket. At the dinner at the end of 1960 given for Lancashire Second XI winning the Minor Counties championship, we were given fixtures for the following year and asked which games we could play in. I said I was available for any. "Fine," said Stan Worthington, "we'll see you next year, Jack." Then my father died, I turned professional and not one invitation came. I often think that becoming a professional in the Leagues turned Lancashire off me.

I had had an offer in 1960 to turn professional with Kearsley, a Bolton team, but my father said I was too young. I'd had one or two upsets at Enfield, particularly the year I got my 50 wickets and 434 runs when I would be put down to number six or seven in the order and didn't bowl in a couple of games. A lot of people suggested it might be jealousy because the captain, Jack Riley, was a bowler, too, but I didn't really think so. But there had to be something wrong. Dad would watch from a friend's car and I went to him one game when we were chasing runs. He suggested I should get my pads on. "You're batting three, aren't you?" he asked. I said no, I was at seven. He watched every game after that and right at the end of the season he asked if I could get in touch with Baxenden, a Ribblesdale League club who had asked me earlier in the season if I would become their professional. "Then we'll have another chat," he said. I was offered £2 10s a match with another ten shillings expenses, which was as much as I was getting for working five days at the brickyard. But dad never saw me play as a professional for he died that winter. He was a very quiet, unassuming man. He only hit me once in my life and I probably only had the highest regard for him after he died.

It was as well I left Enfield, I think, for on another occasion I had refused to bowl against Bacup which was bad. I hadn't been asked to bowl until Bacup had got to about 150 with only two out so I turned my back and walked off to a fielding position. Conrad Hunte was the professional then and in the dressing room after, although he didn't mention any names, said somebody had refused to bowl and if the team was going to run on an individual basis it wouldn't succeed. The captain said a few words but he mentioned me and I felt after that he probably took it out on me a bit. I never refused to bowl again and Conrad taught me a lesson there.

I had the good fortune to have a player called Tommy Barnes as my captain at Baxenden when I started there in 1961. He had been one of the best Lancashire League players and helped create a happy dressing room atmosphere. I did all right bowling at the start but in five knocks I don't think I scored above fifteen. I was able to pick my place in the batting order as the professional and I kept asking to go further and further down the order as I lost my confidence. I arrived for one game and Barnes said: "Right, you're not going to wait, Jack. Put your pads on and open." I argued about it but he stuck to his guns as captain so I went in and finished up getting a hundred, and another hundred the week after. Since then I have never lacked confidence as a batsman. I know some professionals in the leagues think they are the bees knees but you weren't allowed to feel that way at Baxenden where everybody contributed. If there were team fines for being late or getting "ducks" nobody was left out and one chore the team had to do was raise the wooden covers on the team-room windows on the other side of the ground from the pavilion. The player who was last in the ground got that job and it was never between anybody else but Bill Tattersall, a portly player, and me. We often reached the ground about the same time, but being a good deal younger I beat him to the pavilion so he put them up more times than me. I had four good years with Baxenden, winning the championship once, and I was a bit sad when I came to leave. Baxenden were losing money and had none to pay a professional in 1965 so it was good to get an offer from Barnoldswick, of £3 a match, and stay in the Ribblesdale League, which I enjoyed.

During my first year at Baxenden I had played a couple of second-team games with Northamptonshire that had come to nothing. My sister Betty's husband, Peter, worked there at the time and he organised the trial for me. In my first match, against Derbyshire in 1961, I played alongside Colin Milburn, David Larter and Dennis Brookes, who was also the coach.

After bowling one over, Dennis said to me: "There were two leg breaks, two off breaks, a seamer and a googly in that over, Jack." He encouraged me to mix them up like that whereas Stan Worthington had always insisted you had to bowl one way or the other.

During my days at Enfield there was a little fellow, Bobby Marshall, known as Mister Enfield, a local baker for the Co-op who had taken a liking to me and took me to Blackpool over about three or four years playing as an amateur on Sundays. I would collect my money from the Sunday paper round and get the bus for Blackpool from the Load of Mischief pub in Clayton-le-Moors. The great part was that he would bring me some lunch — absolutely magnificent pork and beef pies about four inches thick with lovely pastry — that he used to make. I think I used to look forward as much to having my lunch with Bobby as I did playing cricket. All this helped me play more cricket and on better wickets and against better sides and helped me improve my game. It also opened up a new avenue for me in meeting people in Blackpool and this helped me when I came to leave Barnoldswick to become Blackpool professional in 1968. They say Steve Davis can't think of anything but snooker. Well, I was the same with cricket with all the encouragement I got. Though not as good! Bobby was very disappointed when I left Enfield but we kept in touch and I would still go to Enfield when I could; I still regard it as my home club, and always will.

In my final year as Barnoldswick's professional I acted as substitute pro for Blackpool twice, once taking five wickets in a match with Morecambe who also had a substitute professional in David Hughes, who I was later to join at Old Trafford. It was the first time I had seen him, a good left-arm spinner and a reasonable batsman, but what made me feel he was going to be a top-class player was his fielding. He was absolutely brilliant and kept that standard up through the years. Blackpool became interested in signing me as professional and when Barnoldswick heard that, they offered me a new contract midway through the season. I signed a two-year contract with the proviso that if Blackpool, and only Blackpool, wanted me, I could go. Three or four weeks later Blackpool did come along, a dream for somebody like me, joining a club that had had several Test players. Barnoldswick happily released me but on one condition, that if ever I went back into the Ribblesdale League, Barnoldswick would have first option on my services as a professional, a condition that, as far as I'm concerned, still stands today, nearly twenty years on. I was a bit frightened joining Blackpool, wondering if I was getting out of my depth. But I couldn't refuse, I had to take the chance. If you never attempt to get any higher you don't know what you can achieve. We had practice games at the start of the season and I was soon made to feel better when I got a hundred against a strong Central Lancashire League team. A second hundred followed in another friendly, 90 in my first league match and I think I got another hundred soon after that. All that was enough to get me into the Northern League team that played the Ribblesdale League where I got three wickets, scored 80 odd runs, and it was my good fortune that Buddy Oldfield, the Lancashire coach, was in the crowd. I really have always believed that somebody up there likes me, too.

In 1968 at the age of twenty-seven, I was invited for more trials with Lancashire. My job as a draughtsman, now at County Hall in Bamber Bridge, near Preston, was secure, I was professional with Blackpool and there were no risks going to play for Lancashire Second XI again. The most pleasing part was being asked to pick up Clive Lloyd, who was then professional with Haslingden in the Lancashire League, and take him to Derby, too, for his first game as he started a twelve month qualification period. His presence alone in the dressing room lifted everybody. I know it had an effect on me, helping me to get runs and, something that pleased me more, wickets. The captain was the wicketkeeper, Keith Goodwin, who thought I was in the game just as a batsman. It was a nice, easy-paced wicket and Peter Lever said: "Why not bowl Jack?" "I didn't know he could," replied Goodwin, who said at the end of that first session after I'd bowled that with more practice they could make me into an all-rounder. The next game was against Warwickshire Second XI at Nelson, one of the top Lancashire

League clubs where Learie Constantine and Ray Lindwall had played. It was a slow, wet wicket, soft and offering a bit of spin, the sort of wicket that had all the professionals in the team complaining, but which suited me because it was just what I was used to. I got five wickets and in the second innings, after we had lost two wickets for not many runs, I got 93 in 103 minutes and shared a stand of 145 in 100 minutes with Graham Atkinson, who had joined Lancashire from Somerset. I took three more wickets in the second innings to finish with a match return of eight for 108 in 49 overs so the year was really blossoming as far as Jack Simmons was concerned.

The authorities at Old Trafford thought I needed more pressure put on me so I played against Yorkshire Second XI at Scarborough, took three wickets in each innings, got another 90, and moved up to play with the first team against the Lancashire League at Old Trafford. I didn't get to bat or bowl in the first innings and it was then that word came down from the committee room to the captain, Keith Goodwin again, to put me in at number three and let me bowl a while. I scored 50, took three wickets and was invited to go to Essex, Glamorgan and Blackpool with the first team. Unfortunately I was injured and missed the first two games but was able to make my debut on my home ground at Blackpool against Northants where I started my first-class career with one and a "duck," but took two wickets and got my invitation to join the staff for the start of the 1969 season.

I was sorry to leave Blackpool. I had enjoyed my days there and my affection for the town had been greatly increased by the players introducing me to a magnificent fish and chip shop, The Cottage, where the fish were like whales and everything fresh and hot. It became part and parcel of going to Blackpool to visit The Cottage for what is still one of my favourite meals. I became such a regular customer that once I had made the grade as a Lancashire player they asked me for a photograph to put up in the chip shop alongside many of the stars that performed in the summer theatres. The proprietors there have always been good friends and helped me in my benefit year by giving me a big salmon which I didn't know whether to eat or raffle. In the end

I decided it had better go in the raffle when we had the benefit game at Blackpool.

During the 1960s I played football as a part-time professional in the Lancashire Combination with Great Harwood. I signed when I was nineteen. Others who came to the club under Derek Keighley's chairmanship were Dave Freeman from Chipping, Jack Waring, Hughie Ness, and former Blackburn Rovers players Ken Clayton and John Bray who was also manager. Other managers included George Smith, ex-Manchester City, and Johnny Morris, formerly with Manchester United. We won the Combination championship with about 160 goals with Freeman, a stocky powerhouse of a player, and me both getting over 40 each. That same year we won the Lancashire Floodlit Cup in a two-legged game against Netherfield in which the scores were level going into the closing minutes. I hadn't played well and expected to be substituted, then two minutes from time, the left-winger crossed, I hit it with my left foot and we'd won.

I played for Great Harwood for about eight years and broke my leg three times and an arm once. Cricket was always my first love and when the cricket season started I stopped playing football on Saturdays but continued to play midweek. One of the midweek games was against Morecambe, whose goalkeeper was not being retained and who got out of the way of a 50-50 through ball which I chased just before half time and managed to score. Freeman and I had a reputation for not holding back and we decided in the second half we would play long balls over central defenders and see what the goalkeeper would do. I got one ball that was a good chase, I nearly got there, but the full back tackled me, I went in the air and landed with my arm behind my back. It was broken at the top, an injury that put me out of cricket for about ten weeks, a big disappointment because I had started my second season with Baxenden really well.

Two years later Freeman went for a ball against Horwich and a clash laid out the goalkeeper. The centre half started abusing Dave so I told him to pick on somebody his own size. He did, caught me just right, and I hobbled off in time to go to hospital in the same ambulance as the goalkeeper. The broken leg was put in plaster and when it was taken off I went to the ground to watch a game, slipped in the rain and cracked it again in the same place. This time, it was in plaster for six weeks. The following year, after I had watched us draw a Cup game with Padiham, the chairman said I must play in the replay. I hadn't been cleared for insurance purposes but he said he would cover all that and so I played and scored a hat-trick. The headlines read: "Simmons back with a hat-trick" and when I went to see the specialist the following day to be cleared he shouted from his desk: "What are you here for?" When I told him he said "What about the headline," glanced at my leg and signed the form. When the leg was broken a third time I asked the doctor if I was brittle boned. "No, just bloody unlucky," he said.

3

MY FIRST YEAR – MY FIRST MEDAL

Lancashire cricket went through a difficult time in the 1960s. Nothing much seemed to be going right for them. They finished runners-up to Yorkshire in the championship in 1960 but then fell away so badly that they couldn't get above eleventh place in the next seven years. There were five captains in the 1960s: Bob Barber, who moved to Warwickshire, Joe Blackledge, who was taken out of league cricket and stayed just one season, Ken Grieves, Brian Statham and then Jack Bond. The club had even advertised in *The Times* for a captain and everything came to a head in 1964 when the committee was thrown out at a special meeting of members. Lancashire had last won the championship — well, shared it — in 1950 and had gone too long without winning anything. Bond lifted them to sixth in the championship in his first season as captain in 1968 but it was the introduction of the John Player League the following summer that really started Lancashire's revival and led to that glorious period in which six trophies were won in seven years including the double of John Player League and Gillette Cup in 1970.

When the John Player League was introduced in 1969 it came in for a lot of criticism from older players who wouldn't regard it as cricket, more a razzamatazz type of competition. I thought a lot of teams in those early days treated the Sunday league like a benefit game and it was individuals, more than whole teams, who wouldn't take it seriously, especially, as I say, older players who regarded it with a lot of suspicion. They tried when they were batting and bowling but when it came to fielding they weren't going to throw themselves about, they weren't going to dive just to save a run. But Lancashire placed an emphasis on fielding and Jack Bond was mainly responsible for the team's positive approach to the new game. Experienced players in other teams tended to think it was a way of passing four or five hours on a Sunday and what they didn't do in a championship game, they weren't likely to do on a Sunday, like diving to save runs. Yet Bond always emphasised this: "If you dive and get grass stains on your trousers and can't get them off I'll pay to have them cleaned." The knowledge of how to score runs — and how to save runs come to that — wasn't there in those early games. Batting was usually in championship style or slog, no inbetween, scurrying through for a few more singles, then hitting out blindly. Our emphasis on fielding seemed to place us so far above other teams it just wasn't true and we found ourselves outplaying some teams simply by the runs we saved in the field.

It took until about the middle of the season before people — and that included players — realised that this game was here to stay because of the crowd appeal. People were flocking to grounds and Old Trafford was soon bulging with people wanting to see for themselves the excitement of Sunday afternoons. And if you cannot play in front of big crowds, then you never will perform. You could still get somebody like Brian Close at Yorkshire saying it was six days of playing cricket straight in the proper way, and then on the seventh day — slog. But when he went out there he wasn't one of the players who didn't try. The game took hold of you, especially a young side like we had at Lancashire, and people flocked to it. They loved it. And winning was enough to carry you along on the wave. The more you won, the more you wanted to, and a successful side was just swept along by the game, by winning, and by the enthusiasm of the people watching.

Lancashire's first two games in the new competition in 1969 were at Hove and Chelmsford. We travelled from Oxford to Hove that first weekend and while I played in the game against the University I wasn't in the John Player side that took on Sussex. Nor were one or two others come to that, including opening batsman Graham Atkinson, who was never to play in the John Player League, and David Hughes, a spinner like myself. Farokh Engineer moved up the batting order to open the innings and Clive Lloyd, who had spent the previous year qualifying, was allowed to play though a West Indies tour was just starting. There were 5,000 people at Hove for that first game which was an indication of the public's feeling for the 40-over competition before it had even started. Sussex were all out for 158 with a couple of panic run-outs at the death, and a sign of things to come arrived when Clive scored 59 not out for us and steered us home with five wickets to spare. Clive couldn't play in the next match at Chelmsford but even he would have been hard pressed to have helped us after Essex had charged to 265 for six, a total that was to stand as the highest against Lancashire for the first thirteen years of the John Player League. There were three 50s in that innings but it was Keith Boyce, the West Indian, who showed what could be accomplished by hitting 50 ferocious runs in twenty-three minutes with two sixes and seven fours. Ken Shuttleworth got away with 28 runs in his eight overs but John Sullivan, who was to become such an important part of Lancashire's one-day team, was absolutely murdered, being hit for 73 runs. And that, after more than 250 games since, is still the biggest number of runs, by a fair way, that any Lancashire bowler has given away. Not surprisingly, I suppose, we lost that game by a massive 108 runs after Boyce had taken the wickets of Engineer and Harry Pilling in his first two overs.

Huge though that defeat was, it marked a turning point for Lancashire — and for Jack Simmons. I came into the team for the next game, against Nottinghamshire in the first John Player match at Old Trafford, and since then I have missed only a handful of games and played more than any other player at Old Trafford, although David Hughes has run me a close second. I started with a "duck," Engineer got 46, Hughes hit 38, but I made up for it as a bowler by taking three for 19 as we won by 47 runs. That was the start of a winning run of nine matches which was ended only by the game against Yorkshire being abandoned as we neared the end of the season. It made everybody realise that the John Player League was here to stay and Lancashire were setting the pace, showing what fielding was all about like defending a total of only 130 against a strong Surrey team at Old Trafford and winning by four runs. Such was the pressure then, I remember coming off the field with a headache. One of the most memorable matches in that winning run came against Kent at Blackheath at the end of June when we were top and they were second. We have only twice had a curfew at Lancashire and that game saw one of them when we stayed at the Clarendon Court Hotel in Maida Vale in London. Everybody had to be in the hotel by 11p.m. and in bed by 11.30. I remember breaking it, although I did get permission to go down the Edgware Road to eat at a Chinese restaurant after Harry Pilling and I had arrived late. The outfield at Blackheath was so bumpy we thought the moles had been at it and everybody got hands, body, head behind the ball when fielding. It didn't stop one ball hitting a mole-hill and jumping over Sullivan's head to go for four. We won that game by 20 runs but only after Stuart Leary, who also played football for Charlton Athletic, had hit four sixes and threatened to win the game on his own.

Another memorable game in that winning streak came at Southport two weeks later, one that taught Lancashire a lesson as the small ground heaved under the weight of a crowd of over 10,000. It was our only home game away from Old Trafford and since then we have played only the occasional match away from Manchester. It was an amazing day. The queue to get in stretched more than 250 yards, five deep, and was still there half an hour after the start, when thousands gave up and headed for home where they could watch the game on television. They were eight deep in places in the small ground, people standing on tip-toe, stretching to see a game which made such an enormous impression, because of television coverage. That was the day, I think, when it really got home to people that Lancashire were again a force to be reckoned with. We were playing Glamorgan, a tremendous side in those days, so good under Tony Lewis that they won the County Championship. Obviously, they were capable of stretching even the best teams, yet we bowled them out for 112 with the wickets being shared among five bowlers, Sullivan taking a wicket first ball and finishing with figures of 4-4-0-2. Majid Khan, who was Majid Jahangir then, was in brilliant form after thrashing the West Indies for 147 runs before lunch only the previous week, when Glamorgan were 19 for four and facing a total of over 400. He scored 42 against us but nothing could deny a win for Lancashire then and with Engineer in absolutely dazzling form we won by nine wickets with nearly 16 overs to spare. We nearly won without losing a wicket, only David Lloyd was out five runs away from victory. I most remember Ossie Wheatley, the Glamorgan opening bowler, saying in his nice Welsh accent to Farokh after the game: "I really don't mind you charging me, Farokh, but I am a fast bowler. Do let me set off first." It was a great scene at Southport that day with people jammed up to the fencing, but if they had all been at Old Trafford there could have been more people and they would all have been much more comfortable.

That win gave us a seven point lead at the top of the table, and although we lost to Hampshire at Old Trafford in front of 12,000 people, we won the title in the next-to-the-last game at Nuneaton, another small ground, where we beat Warwickshire by 51 runs. It was a nice little ground, with marquees and another big crowd, and Warwickshire had a pretty good side that included our old captain, Bob Barber, as well as Billy Ibadulla, Rohan Kanhai, John Jameson, Mike Smith, Dennis Amiss, Tom Cartwright, David Brown and Lance Gibbs. There were not many stronger teams in the country and our total of 204 for five was well within their range. Clive Lloyd had returned to us after playing with the West Indies and he and John Sullivan put on 105 in 18 overs with Clive hitting four sixes. There was a row of forms at mid-wicket at Nuneaton, close to the beer tent which had great queues so that men were returning with three or four pints at a time. Clive hit a huge six and several men on one of the forms leaned back to watch it and they all fell over, all on their backs, beer all over the place, trying to watch the ball finishing up in somebody's garden. I took one wicket that day, that of Barber who took a mad swing at me, like a number ten batsman, and was bowled. That was the way a lot of good players played in those days, losing patience and lashing out as if they had to get six every ball. Clive was at his peak as a fielder then and when he was in the covers nobody took a chance if the ball was within two or three yards of him. But Kanhai did, taking him on, beating him by the skin of his teeth before Clive had the last word, catching him off Peter Lever's bowling as we went on to win comfortably. Hampshire finished second that year and their defeat by Essex that day at Portsmouth guaranteed us the title, which meant a great big celebration that night in the hotel in Hagley Road, Birmingham, where we were staying. And on Monday we had to bat against Warwickshire in the championship match at Edgbaston! Not surprisingly, we didn't do too well, and were bowled out for 146 with only Clive making runs and the rest of us collapsing in a heap. Barry Wood opened for us, made one or two absolutely marvellous shots before he was caught in the slips for a "duck".

Our last game in the John Player League that season was one of the funniest I have ever played in. It was played at Worcester and was on television and as there was a prize of £250 for the fastest televised 50 of the season we decided to go all out for it. It didn't matter whether we won or lost, seeing we had already won the championship, but at least we could get the extra prize money to add to the £1,000 we had won as champions, and £600 for the twelve matches we had won. Everybody had to go out there to try to get the fastest 50, everyone but one, David Lloyd, who had to open and be the anchor man. Worcestershire had scored only 158 and when we batted everybody but David Lloyd had a slog with only Sullivan, with 33, getting anywhere near. We finished up with 156 for six in 40 overs, having lost by two runs, and with poor old David Lloyd having batted all the way through for 64 and getting all the blame for us not winning. It gave us a good laugh, although I don't know whether David was too amused.

An outstanding member of our team that year was Ken Higgs. He was an England Test bowler and one of the tightest bowlers I have ever seen. Nobody got runs off him easily and in that year he took 26 John Player wickets, one of the significant factors in our success. Yet I most remember him for two amazing overs in the championship, against Warwickshire and Yorkshire when we were facing defeat. Warwickshire had just under an hour and a half — 33 overs as it turned out — to get 99 runs to win and went into the last over needing five runs and with five wickets standing. Higgs bowled Tom Cartwright and Eddie Hemmings, and Jimmy Stewart came in with a runner for the last two balls and with two runs needed and couldn't score. Unbelievably, a similar finish happened just over five weeks later when we played Yorkshire, who had only to score 65 in 19 overs to win. They got to the last two overs needing one run and with Barrie Leadbeater and Doug Padgett together. Peter Lever bowled a maiden over to Padgett and Higgs, in the final over, took the wickets of Leadbeater, Don Wilson and Richard Hutton without conceding a run, leaving the scores level. You'd have thought we'd won that game if you'd been in the dressing room after the finish, although Yorkshire got an extra five points from the game because they were batting at the end. In that game I got the most illustrious "duck" I have ever scored after joining Jack Bond at the crease. He insisted that I just stay there although I argued that runs were as important as time and I batted 75 minutes for nought. I middled everything, never edged a ball that would have given me a single to third man or fine leg. I was batting number ten that day and when it was nearing tea, Bill Alley, one of the umpires, told me to make sure I didn't get out. If I did, nine wickets would be down and tea would be delayed. He didn't like that. But I did get out, bowled leg stump by a yorker from Chris Old ten minutes before tea, and as I passed Alley on my way to the pavilion, he just looked at me and said: "Bloody idiot!"

That, of course, was my first season with Lancashire and one of my clearest memories is of being overawed facing players of the calibre of John Edrich, Barry Richards, Asif Iqbal, Tom Graveney and Colin Cowdrey. The first time I bowled to Hampshire's Roy Marshall the lads told me: "Now he does give it a whack." I did know of him because I remembered him from my days in the Lancashire League when he was at Lowerhouse. The first three overs I bowled to him were maidens so I went to whoever was fielding at mid-off and said: "I thought you said this man could hit it." Next over, Marshall twice put me over the sightscreen.

One of my other outstanding memories is for quite a different reason! We were involved in a good deal of travelling in June and one of our journeys took us from Swansea to Tunbridge Wells one Friday night. A Richard Burton film was being made in Tunbridge Wells at the time so the town was crowded and the hotel we were staying in had put us into the annexe. We arrived well after midnight and Graham Atkinson, my roommate, pulled back the bedclothes to reveal cockroaches on the bed. The place was filthy and there was damp under the bed, too. It finished up with Graham and our scorer, Mac Taylor, sitting in chairs round the table all night, their trouser bottoms tucked into their socks. I wasn't that squeamish. I took everything off the bed, shook it, then laid down and went to sleep. When I wakened in the morning there they were, still sitting round the table, a wonderful way to prepare for a championship match. That night we went to Peterborough for the John Player match and spent Sunday and Monday nights in a London hotel, travelling each morning to Tunbridge Wells after booking out of the hotel there. I reckon that, starting from Swansea on the Friday, we travelled something like 500 miles across country in three successive evenings. Happily, the computer seems to have got rid of such travelling now and taken that much hassle out of the John Player League.

During that John Player match at Peterborough I dived for a catch at mid-off and hit the ground hard with my hand as I took it. I had to go to hospital on the Monday morning and as I had broken a bone the doctor said he would have to put my hand in plaster. I insisted on him bandaging it so I could continue to play against Kent and, more importantly, go to Lord's for my first-ever game there. But I was sent home on the Tuesday and was really disappointed in having to miss Lord's. I should have been out for three weeks but after only ten days I was watching the game against Warwickshire when somebody left the field injured and, as I was the only one around, I had to take his place. Jack Bond decided to hide me in the field at fine leg and mid-off but Rohan Kanhai found me with a head-high drive which I had to attempt to catch. I did hold on to the ball, but didn't it hurt! The pain soon went so I decided to put myself up for selection in the next game seeing that I could get hurt even being twelfth man.

It was during those early years, in a festival match against Yorkshire at Tewkesbury, that the nickname of Flat Jack was introduced. I had bowled with a flat trajectory in the leagues because the ball would always turn on those wickets, and I can't recollect ever throwing the ball up. Tony Nicholson, the Yorkshire opening bowler, was making the loudspeaker announcements at Tewkesbury and when I went on to bowl he introduced me as "Flat Jack," a name that has stuck ever since.

4
THE DOUBLE

Winning the John Player League in 1969 in its first season gave us at Lancashire the confidence to do even better. And sure enough, 1970 was to prove our best season in years, perhaps even Lancashire's best ever seeing we stayed in the hunt for cricket's three titles right into September, winning two of them. Success in one just kept us going in the others and 1970 was to prove the first year in our domination of the Gillette Cup and all those years in the 1970s when we just kept going back to Lord's.

We hadn't done so well in the Gillette in 1969, knocked out in the second round, and by Yorkshire of all people in front of our own crowd. We batted first and lost that match because we got off to such a slow start from Barry Wood and David Lloyd. When Wood was out in the 17th over he had scored three! Yet when he came back into the dressing-room he thought he'd done a good job. We had been going scatty watching them — we were left virtually playing a 40-over game while our opponents were in a 60-over game. They said the wicket was difficult but when you haven't lost a wicket and runs aren't coming so easily you have got to start taking a few chances. Lloyd could accelerate but Wood often seemed unable to. He would assess a wicket in his own mind — a 150 wicket, a 200 wicket or maybe many more. Most times he would get it right but if he was wrong we were lost. He wouldn't take any risks and when we complained he would say: "You can go in now and get four or five an over. The hard work is done." And we would say: "You're the batsman. If you can't get two runs an over how can we, who are inferior batsmen, get twice as many?" He wouldn't take risks in those first 20 overs but if the openers then got out with not many runs scored, it didn't give the following batsmen time to have a look at the ball and they were put under pressure. If one of them could go on and become the sheet anchor we would get 220 or 250. We would have a few arguments and Woody would fly off the handle and say it was a bad wicket and we would still win. Often he was right, but he did annoy us at times. Yorkshire had no difficulty beating us that day, but that was to prove our last defeat in the Gillette for four years.

The game, in 1970, that started our great run came at Bristol against Gloucestershire, a team we were to have many tussles with, but one we could always beat. I got 14 not out in about two overs as we knocked up 278 for eight and they got off to a good start with Ron Nicholls hitting 75. They were 141-2 at one stage and then I got three wickets — David Shepherd, West Indian Whiteley Phillips, a hard-hitting batsman, and Mike Procter, who came in at number six. We cut them down to 156 for six but they got to 251 and I had three for 39 which I thought gave me a chance of Man of the Match. My three wickets had helped change the course of the game, but the award went to Nicholls.

We easily beat Hampshire in the third round at Old Trafford but it was the semi-final against Somerset at Taunton where I experienced for the first time what a big part nerves can play. Roy Virgin got runs against us, as he often did, Barry Wood took three wickets and although we only needed 208 to win we slipped to 130 for five. We were in the old pavilion with its old-fashioned easy chairs in the dressing room, but I don't think anybody was sitting down. In fact, I don't think anybody was even watching as Jack Bond and John Sullivan shared in the partnership that pulled us round. I was next man in and nervous as hell just pacing around and waiting, but Sullivan played magnificently and we won by four wickets.

Our first final was against Sussex, a strong batting side including Mike Buss who used a very heavy bat and started to lay about us with it. I can remember going on to bowl and being worried about him, but I went round the wicket, on Jack Bond's advice, and bowled him. Jim Parks, Tony Greig and Peter Graves were as good as any other county's middle order but they were all bowled by David Hughes, who bowled really well that day and finished with three for 31. In those days Bond would do what no other captain dared to do, give the last over to a spinner. I remember Hughes bowling it in a semi-final against Kent at Old Trafford and I caught John Shepherd on the mid-wicket boundary as he threatened to beat us. He also bowled the last over in a game against Essex at Chelmsford and Ray East went for a big hit off him, only for David Lloyd to catch it on the boundary edge, put it in his pocket and walk off. Harry Pilling was made Man of the Match in our first final for his 70 not out, a really sound innings. You always felt good when Harry was there although you wouldn't find him hitting over the top or going for sixes. He just gave you so much confidence and I don't think a lot of people gave him the recognition that was due for our success in one-day cricket.

We made a marvellous start in the John Player League by winning nine of the first ten games, but we felt we had been cheated in the one we lost, against Kent at Beckenham. It was our third match and as we were the champions we were the team everybody had to beat. We knew there was going to be a chance of rain so we had to get runs and I was sent in at number three to slog — or should I say in my case, to play shots! I could be sacrificed in our efforts to get quick runs and in 35 overs we managed 202 for seven, which wasn't a bad score. Rain was threatening and Kent played shots from the start, knowing if we could only play ten overs they had to score 58 to win the match. They got their 58 in nine overs and walked off, yet the rules stated that the side batting second had to face ten overs for it to constitute a match. The rain was beating down at the time and had been for two or three overs when Kent went off. There was no consultation as Colin Cowdrey, who had just hit a six off Ken Shuttleworth, led the dash for the pavilion. We didn't say anything and went off knowing the match hadn't been finished although they had got the required number of runs as if it had been a ten-over game. We were drenched but we were happy as we weren't able to get out again and we thought the game was a draw, a view held by the umpires as well. Yet, for the only time in history, the rules were changed after a game to say that if a score was attained in less than the ten overs then the game was over. So the result was changed and Kent were awarded the points. This made us all the more determined to win and a mock cup — of cardboard, I think — was sent to Kent with the message: "You still won't win the Cup so take this. It's as near as you'll get." Mind you, I think the rule does make more sense now, but at the time the side batting second had to have ten overs for it to constitute a match. And Kent didn't.

Sullivan's importance in the one-day game was shown in all sorts of ways but particularly with his hard-hitting batting, such as his innings against Leicestershire when he was out for 43, bowled by Ray Illingworth off the 14th ball he received. Illingworth had figures of 4-0-38-1 and I don't recall him ever having been hammered in such a way. It says something for "Sully" that he even outscored Clive Lloyd that day. Sullivan came more into his own in the John Player League. He was a must in the number five or six position and I thought he had great ability as a bowler and was very underestimated. He was a match-winner. He might not have been technically correct but he was such a good striker of the ball with a remarkable eye and fine timing, the ideal middle-order batsman. Maybe it was the way he had to play in that type of cricket that didn't impress the Lancashire selectors that he was a man who could play a long innings in the County Championship. He didn't get as many runs as his talent deserved but then he probably didn't get enough chance in the championship to learn to adjust from one type of game to the other. But when runs had to be scored quickly it was Sullivan who had to go in, always the scapegoat, the sacrificial lamb. Bond regarded him highly as a team man and was determined to get him capped, which he did. We always regarded those late middle-order positions as Kamikaze batting although Wood thought we were the glory boys, a few quick runs and we'd made a name. He once had to bat in the middle with a few balls remaining in a John Player game against Derbyshire at Buxton. He ran down the wicket, had a big heave and the ball flew very high and was caught by Ian Buxton. So whenever he used to go out needing quick runs we would tell him to give it the Buxton blast.

Clive Lloyd, who had played only half the season for us in

1969 due to the West Indies tour, was with us all the time in 1970 and I particularly remember one shot at Cardiff when he hit a ball from Don Shepherd, the Glamorgan off-spinner, over the poplar trees. It was still going up when it cleared the trees and Shepherd, who finished with one for 52 in eight overs, applauded the shot. And you don't get a bowler doing that very often. In those days Clive was a similar type to Gary Sobers, an all-round cricketer whose fielding was second to none, an outstanding batsman, and a very useful bowler. He bowled a lot then, before his knees went, and not just as one of the make-weights but a regular bowler when the conditions suited him. He even opened the bowling in a Gillette Cup final which is a fair indication of how much he was valued. He didn't use his great height like Joel Garner but he was able to move the ball, he had a whippy action and was a little bit quicker at times than people anticipated.

We were so confident then that we knew the teams we would beat. It was often not a question of *if* we could win, but by how many, and we won most of our matches with great ease. The key was in the balance of the side, the stroke makers, strikers of the ball, all-rounders and good bowlers. On top of all that we had the best fielding side of all time. The John Player League certainly helped me a lot; it was the sort of game I was used to, after all my years in league cricket. It helped me to settle in fairly quickly and allowed me to feel part of the side by small but vital contributions, the sort that might not be rated so much in the championship. It was a great game, it meant excitement, success, and very much looking forward to a game, probably more than any other except the Gillette Cup.

There was no John Player game more exciting than the last one in 1970 when we won the title for the second year running. We had won twelve and lost two of the fifteen matches we had played and the game became even more significant for us as it was against our old enemies, Yorkshire. The gates were closed soon after the start and thousands had to be turned away. The official attendance was 27,559 but it was believed that gate-crashers had taken the real figure beyond 30,000, the highest number at Old Trafford for twenty-two years. Two run-outs helped us and Ken Shuttleworth took three wickets in four balls in the middle of the innings, one of them being Geoff Boycott who scored 81 and then fell to a brilliant catch by Bond at deep backward point, a fantastic catch like his more famous one that dismissed Asif Iqbal in the Gillette Cup final the following year. So Yorkshire scored only 165 and when we were 94 for three in the 24th over, Sullivan made sure there would be no mistakes by hitting 56 in 40 minutes, carrying us through to a seven-wicket win with more than four overs to spare. Harry Pilling scored the winning run, a fitting end for the player who was first to 1,000 runs in the John Player League. He was a great worker of the ball, a placer, a deflector, who kept the ball and the scoreboard moving.

The Gillette Cup six days later gave us the double, but the championship eluded us, although we were in the running right to the end. In those days Ford were giving a car to the first bowler to reach 100 wickets in all competitions and to the batsman who scored the fastest 100. Peter Lever led the way with wickets for much of the season but Tony Buss of Sussex ran him hard and they were neck and neck when Lancashire played Sussex at Blackpool late in August. Buss needed five while Lever was chosen to play for England against the Rest of the World at the Oval. Sussex batted first at Blackpool on the Wednesday which helped, but England, too, batted first in the Test on the Thursday which had to make Buss favourite. We got away to an opening stand of 265 between Wood and David Lloyd but Buss bowled on and on, for 42 overs to take six wickets for 117 runs. Bond was the fifth of Buss's wickets, the one that won Sussex the car, and as soon as he was out, Buss hugged the catcher, Peter Graves, then set off running round the field with all the other players chasing him. They celebrated that night and the following day we bowled them out inside 40 overs to win by an innings. We had at one time in our own innings got enough runs perhaps to have declared, but Jack Bond would never do that sort of thing. Then Lever took seven wickets for England to also reach 100! Still, I don't know how we would have divided the car.

Although we did well in the championship, it never seemed

firm in our minds, at least not in mine, the way the John Player and the Gillette were. We played Warwickshire after the Sussex game and got to the end needing 179 to win in 26 overs and we only stopped going for them when there were only one or two overs to go. Lance Gibbs, their West Indian off-spinner, bowled two overs at the end and took three wickets for one run to give Warwickshire victory by 31 runs. One of his wickets was mine, caught off bat and pad though I didn't hit it. The last wicket was that of Ken Shuttleworth and he said he didn't hit it either and both of us had been given out by the same umpire. We felt they had not been good decisions and we said to Jack Bond that he should be marked down and given poor marks on the captain's report on the umpires. Bond taught me something that day by refusing to mark that night but waiting until the following day and then assessing the umpire properly over the three days. When I became captain of Tasmania, and at times of Lancashire, I learned not to mark in the heat of the moment.

We went to Worcester for the next match where their New Zealand opener, Glenn Turner, was heading for the record number of centuries in a season by a Worcestershire player. When he got to 99 in the second innings Bond tried to help him by not having a mid-off, just leaving Clive Lloyd at cover. Turner pushed to mid-off and ran for what should have been an easy single but Clive ran round, picked up the ball and hit the stumps to run him out. It was a shame, but he did get there the following game.

We didn't win any of the last six games, the next to last match being at Cardiff against Glamorgan who finished second that year. Peter Walker attempted to hit me straight for six, only to sky the ball high to mid-wicket where Barry Wood looked up, but couldn't see it as it was very sunny. He wasn't wearing a cap — he seldom did — and just couldn't pick up the ball. Walker went on to get 114 and Glamorgan to 301 for five declared, so we were left the impossible task of getting 137 to win in 13 overs. The Glamorgan opening batsman, Geoff Ellis, had an unfortunate experience in that match, being hit three times on the head by Ken Shuttleworth. He just carried on after the first one, went off for a while after the second, but had to go to hospital after the third. Even though we went through the last six games without winning we still only finished 21 points behind the champions, Kent, and four behind the second team, Glamorgan. Still, we had two trophies to show for the best year Lancashire had ever had. It had been a great year and really, I knew nothing but success in my first years as a county player.

It was during the 1970 season that I scored my first century in county cricket, against Sussex at Hove at the beginning of August. My first 50 for the club had come only two weeks earlier, against Middlesex in my first visit to Lord's when I batted at number nine and helped us move from 232 for seven to 343 for nine declared. Then, when Clive Radley and Norman Featherstone were holding us up with a big partnership, Jack Bond asked me to bowl leg breaks. I broke the stand for my only wicket of the match and we won by ten wickets. Two weeks later at Hove I went in as nightwatchman in the second innings to face one ball and when I was in the 40s the following morning, Jim Parks asked me what my highest score was. I said I'd only had one 50 and he replied: "Well, there'll be more." I wanted to make sure my 50 wasn't just a one-off, that I could get runs, and I got into a very nervous state. Harry Pilling didn't help, for ever taking a single off the last ball. I didn't know this sort of thing went on, with players pinching the bowling, until I got back to the dressing-room and the lads said: "Harry's a good counter, isn't he?" Harry just smiled and said: "You'll be all right." I was about 80 at lunch and Bond told us we had to go for some quick runs. I said: "After I've got my hundred?" And he said: "Oh yes, you can play for that." Once I got to 100 I hit the next three balls for four and then got out. I was exhausted when I went off and wondered then how some batsmen could concentrate so hard for so long all season.

So 1970 was a memorable season not only for Lancashire, but also for me — a truly vintage year.

5

A HAT-TRICK OF GILLETTE CUPS

After just a couple of years in county cricket I had three winners' medals on the mantelpiece — two from the John Player League, and one Gillette Cup. It was amazing. Lancashire had gone for years without winning anything, just a joint share of the County Championship to show for twenty-five years of cricket since the war and now here they were, three Cup wins in two years. The double of Gillette and John Player in 1970 was a really outstanding performance, particularly when you remember that we finished third in the championship that year as well. That was the start of a phenomenal run for Lancashire in the Gillette Cup, a run that was to see us reach six Lord's finals in seven years, four of them as winners, including the hat-trick. What a wonderful feeling it was in 1970 to win through to the final, a great sensation and one of almost total command. Every game seemed to produce a comfortable win and even with the John Player League as well, there were very few cliff-hangers. Of course there were a few nerve-ends jangling but it never got to the extent of getting to the last ball or the last few runs, a game which could go either way. Perhaps it was all too easy.

Then came 1971 with the odd tight game, especially the twilight semi-final match with Gloucestershire at Old Trafford when David Hughes hit 24 runs in an over off John Mortimore to take us through to our second successive final. Our first Gillette game that year was against our semi-final opponents of the previous season, Somerset, with David Lloyd scoring an unbeaten 94 to lead us to a resounding win. The next game, at Worcester, followed a similar pattern although we were tending to get a little over-confident in Gillette matches. We had just lost two Sunday games and in the championship match before the Gillette Cup-tie we had been rained off for three days against Somerset at Bath. Peter Lever, who was senior professional with Harry Pilling, thought it was time for a few home truths and he went through the entire side in the dressing room, picking holes in everybody, obviously a bit fed up with the way we had been playing, not showing enough grit and determination. "Let's see what we're here for," he said. "Are we here to play for Lancashire or are we here just to play for individuals, get selected for England, or get enough runs or wickets just to stay in the side." It all got a bit heated, a few words were exchanged, but at least we all left that meeting ready to analyse ourselves, what we had contributed to the team. Lever accused some players of not pulling their weight so they went out at Worcester determined to show him what they could do. And everything had to be right in that match. One man dominated Worcestershire's innings — New Zealander Glenn Turner who was then still developing into the very good batsman he was to become. When he first went to Worcester he was regarded as an anchor man, but by this time he was coming out of his shell to such an extent that he scored more than half his team's runs. We kept them down to 215 for six but Turner batted right through the innings, a fine display that deserved victory. We did wobble as we lost two quick wickets, but Barry Wood, Clive Lloyd and Farokh Engineer saw us through to what turned out to be quite an easy win and a place in the quarter-final, another away match, this time at Chelmsford, against Essex, a match I will never forget.

What a start we made. Two wickets down for two runs, then 59 for six when I joined Clive Lloyd at the wicket and a quick change of fortune needed. It wasn't easy batting that day. Keith Boyce was bowling with real pace, John Lever was a lot quicker than he is these days, and Stuart Turner was seaming the ball. I've always had a high regard for Turner who has never played for England yet contributed so much to county cricket. I was facing Ray East, their left-arm spinner, when I first went in, a bowler with great flight control. I pushed and pushed at him, then had a slog and got away with it before edging to the wicket-keeper, Brian Taylor, the Essex captain, who, luckily for us, dropped it. It was the change of luck we needed and with Clive playing beautifully to score a great century we were able to pull victory out of the fire and get into the semi-final.

The big controversy of that game was when Essex thought Clive had edged a catch off Lever to the wicketkeeper. Just about every player went up, but Clive didn't move and the umpire, David Constant, didn't think he had hit it. To be very, very truthful, I didn't think he hit it either. Clive said he didn't hit it but the Essex lads took it badly and I think it took some of the joy out of the Essex-Lancashire fixtures for a year or two after that. I've always found Clive the sort of player who walked when he knew he'd hit the ball but whether or not he did hit it, I was amazed at the way the Essex players took it. After all many players, like David Steele and Geoff Boycott, didn't walk and while other players didn't like it, no great song and dance was made about it. When I started playing you could count on one hand the players who didn't walk, but it was getting steadily worse. Anyway, we got over the crucial time, Clive and I shared a partnership of 91 and we got to 203 for nine in the 60 overs. Not a great total but you always felt that once you had got into the 200s you had something to bowl at. We had Essex sinking at 112 for six but Turner was our bugbear, getting 50 and hitting me out of the ground and into the gardens of the houses alongside. They got to the last over needing 13 to win and one thing I have never been able to work out to this day was why David Hughes, our left-arm spinner, bowled that final over. These days nobody would ever think of finishing off with a spinner when only 13 were needed. But Jack Bond, our captain, had faith, not just then but in other games, to bowl Hughes for the last over. It proved to be right because with his second ball he had East caught on the boundary edge by the pavilion to give us victory. Some of the Essex lads had cooled down and accepted the decision about Clive, but others wouldn't have a drink with us after the game. That was their prerogative but if that happened now nothing would be said about it.

That was the first tight Gillette match we had had in seven

games, but now we were to get an even closer one in an Old Trafford Cup-tie that was captured by television and will live on perhaps for ever as one of the greatest Gillette matches of all time. The game started on time and finished at five minutes to nine, the longest one-day game in history and regarded by television as the greatest ever. If anybody is in any doubt, just look at the number of times it is replayed. It was a game that had everything and was really brought to life during Gloucestershire's innings by Mike Procter who scored 65 before he was out, a dismissal that raised a few eye-brows. He was caught down the legside by our wicketkeeper, Farokh Engineer, a magnificent diving catch which many people, including Procter, thought he had dropped, then recovered. I have watched it on television time and time again, about twenty or thirty times, slowed it down, but I can find nothing wrong with the decision. People got upset but the one person who probably didn't feel anything against Engineer was Procter himself, first in to the dressing-room after the game to congratulate us. Gloucester totalled 229 for six and when we slid to 163 for six with all the big guns out and only Jack Bond left when I went in, we were under a good deal of pressure. I faced the first ball from John Mortimore and pushed it back down the wicket. Bond walked down to me and said: "Well, you've played yourself in now, so we'd better start playing a few shots and try to get nearer this total." There was no slogging. We tried to get ones, to keep the score moving with Bond the anchor man, making sure he was in control with whoever came in to join him. We got to 203 before I attempted a very big hit, trying to emulate a shot early in my innings when I had hit Mortimore for six. The only difference this time was that my leg stump was knocked back.

We then needed 27 to win in six overs, difficult enough in ordinary circumstances with Procter still to bowl but even harder in terrible light when Hughes went out at getting up for quarter to nine. I can see him now, walking out to the wicket, looking up into the sky, with the lights of the railway station behind him and the little lights on the scoreboard flashing like spotlights. He was nearly bowled by the first ball from Mortimore which was only an inch away from the off stump.

But that was the little bit of luck we needed. It was about time for Procter to bowl again and Hughes knew it would not be easy to hit him for four or five an over. So he decided to attempt to hit Mortimore, a successful attack which is now history as he hit him for 24 in one over — 4, 6, 2, 2, 4, 6. That was the 56th over and I can still remember being in the pavilion where all the lights were on and, after David had hit the fifth ball for four and we were within seven of winning, I was shouting at the window with one or two others: "Right, you can take your time now! We can get the rest in singles." Then David hit another six which left us with one to get. But Procter charged in from his full run and it took to the fifth ball of that 57th over for Bond to get the winning run.

As I said, Procter was the first into the dressing room to congratulate us. I know he greatly admired Bond's decision to bat on in the poor light and I know, too, that poor old Dickie Bird was getting a little bit worried, with twenty odd thousand people still there and the light deteriorating quite quickly. Still, it had all worked out in the end, at least for Lancashire anyway. I didn't think of it at the time because I was just happy to be back at Lord's, but people reminded me later of the good bowling spell I'd had, two for 25, and the contribution of 25 runs at a difficult time and thought I might have had the Man of the Match award. Maybe in years to come, when people look back on the game, they will think well, yes, there must have been a chance of Jack Simmons winning it. But the pure excitement of that over, the way David Hughes played those shots to take us in six balls from a position where we could lose to the very edge of winning, nobody could think of making anybody else Man of the Match.

So there we were at Lord's again, with a stiffer task than in 1970 as we were now taking on Kent, a pretty formidable side who had been county champions the previous year. We started the match badly, losing Barry Wood before we'd got a run, but there was Clive Lloyd again, loving Lord's, the big occasion, and sharing in a good partnership with David Lloyd that lifted us past 100 with only two wickets down. Clive scored 66, playing shots all round the wicket with some of them over mid-wicket off the front foot that were just out of this world. Even so, it needed a partnership of 45 between David Hughes and myself to give us a reasonably good total of 224 for seven. We didn't half scamper some quick singles, not to mention twos and threes, and I think I even surprised myself, waddling down that twenty-two yards as fast as I could go. We were confident we had a winning score but became even more certain of ourselves when Peter Lever and Ken Shuttleworth grabbed a couple of quick wickets. At 162 for six, Kent looked to be almost finished, except for Asif Iqbal, their Pakistani batsman, who, once he had settled in, completely tore us apart. It didn't matter who Bond put on to bowl, Asif murdered them until his innings was ended by one of the most wonderful catches I have ever seen. They do say that catches win matches and if ever there was one to prove that saying it came in this Gillette Cup final. I was bowling at the time, trying to contain Asif who was going down the wicket to me so quickly I just couldn't tell what he was going to do next. When he wasn't hitting balls on the legside, he was dabbing them down to third man or driving and all I was trying to do was get every ball into the blockhole, just trying to smother the man. Again he came down to me and drove a ball about head high and a yard and a half wide of extra cover. Or so it seemed until Bond took off from that position and caught it as he was flying through the air. He dropped down, threw the ball in the air, and I couldn't believe it. A miraculous catch to end a marvellous innings and Asif trudged off to the dressing room, hardly believing what we had all witnessed. Bob Woolmer was batting at eight then, Bernard Julien was next in, so Kent still had plenty of batting and stroke-making to come. But that wicket, I think, had deflated them, just as it had lifted us and convinced us again that we could win.

Bond's astute captaincy showed when he quickly brought Lever back into the attack and when he dismissed Woolmer with one that came back up the hill — a hell of a good ball — Kent were 199 for eight. The clincher came with the running out of Julien, beaten by a marvellous piece of fielding by Clive who was fielding at mid-wicket and who, in one movement, picked up the ball and threw down the stumps without even getting Farokh Engineer, our wicketkeeper, to play any part. After that there was only Derek Underwood. He had a bit of a whack, was caught by Wood at mid-off, and we had won the game by 24 runs, a bit more comfortably than we had thought with the last four wickets falling for three runs. Asif was quite pleased to be chosen as Man of the Match but in his heart he was deeply disappointed that after such a truly magnificent innings, he had not received a winners' medal as well.

At one stage, the 1971 season had all the promise of being the best-ever in Lancashire's history as we stayed in the running for three trophies right through to the end of the season. We had to settle again for third place in the championship, and although we lost three of the first six John Player League matches, we won seven of the next eight to virtually make sure of the title for the third year running. We were top of the League with Essex when we went into the next-to-the-last match with third placed Worcestershire at Old Trafford. The match was reduced to ten overs after heavy rain and after they had scored 77 for three we could only reach 67 for seven in near-farcical conditions. When we went into our last match, against Glamorgan at Old Trafford, Essex and Worcestershire had completed their programmes and Worcestershire were on top. Our run-rate, the deciding factor if teams were level on points, was superior to Worcestershire, so victory over Glamorgan would make us champions.

On the day before the match Clive Lloyd was married and the reception was held at Old Trafford. All the players were there, conscious of the important match the following day and that all eyes were on them. I know I had only the equivalent of two pints of beer and the players started to leave about 11 p.m. whereas on a normal night they might have gone out, had a few drinks and not bothered too much about the time. But because we felt under the microscope hardly anybody drank at all, and what happened? We lost, and the title went with it! The wicket looked perfect, flat and hard, yet we bowled and fielded so well that we kept them down to 143. I don't think we had ever been more confident of winning but Peter Walker and Majid Khan bowled well to their fields, we blocked and blocked, got behind the scoring rate, and panicked. When I went in to bat at 87 for six, Jack Bond was at the other end. He sent me back when I set off for a single and I slipped. The fielder faltered as well, I got up, slipped again and finished up on my stomach, the only time I remember being out without facing a ball. The wickets just wouldn't stop falling. Four went while we stuck on 87 and we were bowled out for 109. Glamorgan had won by 34 runs, Worcestershire were champions, and we were so depressed in the dressing room that nobody spoke for a time.

It didn't seem all that long before we were defending the Gillette Cup again, trying to make it three in a row in 1972. And who should we meet in the second round after getting a bye in the first — but Somerset again. We had beaten them in the 1970 semi-final and in the first round in 1971 but anybody the least bit superstitious must have thought they were bound to come good this time, third time lucky. But it wasn't to be. We batted first and there was the maestro, Clive Lloyd, leading the way again with 86 in our total of 243 for nine, a pretty good score. Somerset provided great resistance, especially Merv Kitchen, and it was one of the few times I went round the wicket to bowl. I bowled to him quite late in the day when Somerset were threatening to snatch the game and that was one of the best bowling performances I ever had. In those days Flat Jack was renowned for blockhole deliveries but never did I have such a high percentage of balls in exactly the right place. Merv kept digging them out and played well for his 116. But it was not quite good enough and he was close to tears at the end of a game which Somerset lost by only nine runs, the closest encounter we had had with them.

Our quarter-final match with Hampshire at Bournemouth was one of those games that stays vividly in my mind, with one man's innings dominating the day, but again not enough to overcome Lancashire's great teamwork. Hampshire were a particularly fine batting side in those days with Barry Richards and Gordon Greenidge opening, David Turner, Roy Marshall, Richard Gilliat and Trevor Jesty to follow. We looked to be in for a real hammering when Hampshire got to 118 before their second wicket fell, that of Turner whose contribution to a stand of 88 with Richards had been 26. The next few wickets fell fairly quickly but through it all stood Richards, a great batsman who didn't care who bowled to him or how, he just put the ball where the fielders weren't, and hit 129 of their total of 223. I was hit for 55 runs in my 12 overs and I had a chat with Bond about where I should bowl. His advice was always: "If he misses, Jack, you've got to hit, so bowl straight." But Richards was improvising, stepping away and playing as he wanted, so we decided to give him singles with mid-off and mid-on standing back, a deep mid-wicket and deep square leg. Bowl at his leg stump, let him flick it round, and all he'd get was one. Great idea, we thought, to keep the great man quiet. Of course, he soon realised what we were doing. He just smiled, went down the wicket next over and when I bowled leg stump he hit it through extra cover for four like a tracer bullet. Next ball he stepped away a little bit further and hit over extra cover for four more. We decided to put a fielder on the extra cover boundary. Backward point was moved more to cover, the cover fielder went on the boundary and when he again moved away next ball, ready to hit me in the covers, I bowled wide of the leg stump. This one he late cut for four and he must have hit me for 14 or 16 in the over, one of the few times I just haven't known where to bowl. Once he got to 100, Richards went more for slogging, which a player of his great ability didn't need to do. In one over against Peter Lee he just wound up and slogged at every ball and I think he was bowled off the fifth or sixth delivery of the over without having got a run in it. I think he was tired out, but we were highly delighted because they still had seven to ten overs left and he was out for 129. We bowled them out for 233 with ten balls to go which was almost unbelievable after the start they had had. Consistency, the hallmark of the Lancashire side, showed throughout when we batted. Everybody chipped in and Wood got 66 although there was never any chance of him getting Man of the Match after Richards's innings. Still, teamwork had won the day again.

In rather sharp contrast to my own bowling performance, Peter Sainsbury, Hampshire's left-arm spinner, gave away only

29 runs in his 12 overs. David Lloyd, one of the best players of spin bowling as his 214 not out in the Edgbaston Test against India proved, always thought Sainsbury didn't turn the ball sharply and despite his accuracy and consistency he wouldn't rate him highly on his list of spin bowlers. He used to say Sainsbury wasn't as good a bowler as his figures suggested and would go out intent on getting runs against him. Yet time and time again he would get out to him. This was one of those times — c Richards b Sainsbury 17. In one of his last years Sainsbury had over 900 runs and 100 wickets and anybody who can get those sort of figures is no dummy. I went to Rhodesia and South Africa with him and he was just as effective there. Such a nice man, too.

The semi-final brought back memories of the previous season's final with a game against Kent who, I felt in those years, were trying hard to knock us off our perch as champions of one-day cricket. We again batted consistently with Harry Pilling leading the way this time with an innings of 70. I went in with an over to go and got a "duck," but that sort of thing didn't worry me in those days because Bond's policy was that if you were asked to do a job for the side, occasional failure wouldn't result in you being dropped. We scored 224 for six and were a little bit on edge as to whether it would be enough. This was the only game I ever remember getting a bit annoyed with Bond who seemed to be trying all the bowlers except me when Mike Denness and Colin Cowdrey were going along quite well, taking Kent past 100 with only two wickets down. As usual, when he did ask me to bowl, he softened my anger by saying he had saved me because he knew I could curb this player or get that one out. He was saving me — he had a plan! They were 110 for two and we were not too confident until I took the wickets of Denness, Asif and Alan Knott. David Hughes also got three wickets including that of John Shepherd, Kent's West Indian all-rounder, who could hit powerfully. They needed 23 to win with three wickets standing when Shepherd hit the ball towards me on the mid-wicket boundary opposite the pavilion. I thought: "Crikey, Simmo, you can't afford to drop this." It went straight into my hands, out again, over my shoulder and I turned round and caught it. How that happened I just don't know. Kent's last pair, Norman Graham and Derek Underwood, came together with 12 needed for victory but they were still a couple of hits away when Underwood was stumped off Hughes off the last ball of the innings. We had won another close one by seven runs and for the third successive year we were at Lord's, which was fast becoming our second home.

We beat Warwickshire in the final by four wickets, a game that is memorable to me only for Clive's great innings of 126. They were a good side with two dangerous batsmen in Rohan Kanhai and Alvin Kallicharran. Kanhai kept sweeping Hughes, a shot that was to prove his downfall when he was caught on the boundary edge by David Lloyd. Several of us ran over to congratulate Lloyd, we were so relieved to see the back of Kanhai. Their 234 for nine wasn't a bad total and at 26 for two we were in trouble. But Clive launched the most savage attack I have ever seen on fast bowling with David Brown being the most heavily punished as he went for 67 in 12 overs, all due to Clive who repeatedly hit the ball back past the bowler in one of the most memorable innings played in a Lord's final.

6
THREE MORE FINALS

After winning the Gillette Cup for the third successive time in 1972, Jack Bond decided to call it a day. He had been captain for five years, had won five competitions and had brought glorious days back to Lancashire with a hat-trick of Gillette wins and two John Player League titles in its first two years. Nobody was sorrier than me to see him finish for all my years in county cricket had been under his captaincy, years of fairly unbroken success which had given me non-stop pleasure, enabled me to go abroad as a coach, and secured my life as a full-time professional cricketer. He wasn't lost altogether to Lancashire, at least not straightaway, because he became the club's joint coach along with John Savage, following on after Buddy Oldfield who left the club early in the 1972 season. David Lloyd was given the captaincy in succession to Bond and Lancashire immediately fell away in his first year in 1973. I suppose many clubs would have been happy to have finished fourth in the John Player League and to have reached the semi-final of the Benson and Hedges Cup. But for Lancashire it was a mark of failure not to win something, not to at least go again to Lord's which was becoming like a second home to us. We finished twelfth in the championship that summer and in the competition we had come to call our own, the Gillette Cup, we were knocked out in the quarter-final, our first Gillette defeat since 1969.

Our first Gillette match in 1973 was against Bedfordshire at Luton which we won comfortably enough as everybody might have expected. Harry Pilling didn't get to bat as we scored 275 for three but he did have the honour of bowling the last over when Bedfordshire had nine wickets down and didn't have a price of winning. Harry must have hypnotised them for off only the second ball he sent down, the last man was run out — still 127 runs away from our total! That was the day when Yorkshire lost to Durham, the first county to be beaten by a Minor County in the Gillette Cup, and news came over the tannoy system about how badly placed Yorkshire were in the game. How the Lancashire supporters cheered — they loved nothing better than to see the Yorkies put in their place, especially by a Minor County. I must say I really felt sorry for Yorkshire, even though they are our arch enemy. Through the years I have made more friends in the Yorkshire camp than in any other county and I knew how deflated they must have been — I'll bet it was terrible in the dressing room when it was all over.

We had the good fortune to get another Minor County in the second round — Staffordshire — who we beat by six wickets at Old Trafford thanks to a super knock of 85 not out by David Lloyd who put in some good personal performances in his first year as captain. We did go to Lord's again in the Gillette Cup that year, but only to face Middlesex in the quarter-final. We scored 224 for six, thanks mainly to Pilling who scored 90, but Middlesex made a marvellous start to their reply with an opening stand of 135 from Norman Featherstone and Mike Smith. Even so, I thought we had a good chance of winning when wickets started to tumble and even the usually composed Mike Brearley started to panic. As Middlesex were wavering we could see a storm appearing and but for a cloudburst I feel we could have won. But the game was interrupted and it allowed Middlesex time to re-think and compose themselves for the following day when they went on to win by four wickets with one over to spare. There was one small consolation for us that year as Gloucestershire, our opponents in very memorable games in the three previous years — when we beat them each time, of course — went on to win the Gillette Cup by beating Sussex in the final. I know everybody at Lancashire was delighted for them.

We had a little better run in the Benson and Hedges Cup where we demolished Glamorgan in the quarter-final but then lost to Worcestershire in an exciting semi-final of low scores at

Old Trafford. The scores finished level at 159 with Jim Cumbes and Rodney Cass scrambling a leg bye off the last ball and Worcestershire having won by virtue of having lost fewer wickets. Some people also remember the game for the first appearance of John Abrahams who went on as a substitute fielder in the televised match and held two marvellous outfield catches to dismiss Basil d'Oliveira and Norman Gifford.

Still, not to bother. We got back into the swing of the Gillette Cup the following year, 1974, and who should we draw in the first round but the holders, Gloucestershire, at Bristol. We really looked forward to that match at the end of June and after beating them again, by 50 runs this time, we drew Middlesex at Lord's in the next round which had a few hearts fluttering, I can tell you. However, this is the only Gillette match I ever missed. I had had gastro-enteritis just before it and was kept away from the rest of the players before being taken to Lord's in preparation for the second-round game. I badly wanted to play although I was tending to get a little bit light-headed and knew it might not be a good thing if I did turn out. I went training on the morning of the match, had a good run round and came back sweating, then went out again to practise. When I returned to the pavilion I had reached the top of the steps and was about to tell David Lloyd I was fit when he said: "I don't think we'd better risk you, not so soon after being ill in bed." I was blazing mad, thinking how stupid it was to take me all the way to Lord's and then not play me. But after a couple of minutes I quietened down and watched from the dressing room as we scored 193 for nine, and crushed Middlesex by 81 runs.

The quarter-final saw us drawn against Yorkshire at Headingley and we had a terrible first session as we crawled our way to 101 for six off 39 overs. This was the game when I was asked to go in as "lunch watchman!" "Go in and see it to lunch," I was told. "You're expendable. Then try to improve the scoring rate." So I was promoted to number six ahead of John Sullivan and David Hughes and a fat lot of good it did us as I was lbw to Steve Oldham for one. There was a thrilling partnership between Hughes, who again came to the rescue and was the only batsman in the last six to get into double figures, and Clive

Lloyd who loves the challenge of a Roses fixture and came up trumps again with 90 out of 205. Nobody needs to be asked to do anything when we play Yorkshire and we were all on our toes when we fielded, bowling them out for 173 with Lever taking four good wickets. We had them 28 for two before Geoff Boycott and John Hampshire came together in a stand that added 66. Then Lever came back for his second spell, one of the fastest he has ever bowled in a one-day game, to have Boycott caught behind, bowl Hampshire and then have both David Bairstow and Barrie Leadbeater also caught at the wicket by Engineer. They were great wickets and Lever finished with four for 17 in his 12 overs, a performance I know he regards as one of his best. Playing Yorkshire in the Gillette Cup reminds me of the previous time the teams had met in this tournament, in 1969, my first year at the club although I wasn't in the side then. Cyril Washbrook was chairman of the selection committee and he said before the game that all Lancashire had to worry about was John Hampshire. Get him out and the game was as good as won. The only problem, as Jack Bond was fond of recalling in following years, was that they couldn't get Hampshire in! At least not until after Boycott and Phil Sharpe had shared in an opening stand of 137 and Yorkshire had almost sealed the game!

Our semi-final match in 1974 was against Worcestershire, a reminder of our Benson and Hedges match the previous summer. Regardless of that game we always felt in those days that with our batting we could outscore any team and this was no exception after a start of 123 from David Lloyd and Barry Wood. A bit of a setback followed with Frank Hayes and Clive Lloyd going for "ducks" — and you didn't see that happen very often — but 236 for seven wasn't a bad score. I took five for 49 as we won by 28 but again I couldn't get the gold award, though I couldn't really argue with the choice of Barry Wood who scored 91 and bowled his 12 overs for 19 runs.

We were at Lord's again for the only final we took part in that was affected by rain. It really poured down on the Friday, even as we arrived at the Clarendon Court Hotel in Maida Vale just down from the ground. We all thought there was no chance

Above *Enfield cricket team 1904. My grandfather, Bob Simmons, is in the back row, second from the left.*

Below *Another generation of Enfield cricketers — my father is in the middle row, second from the left.*

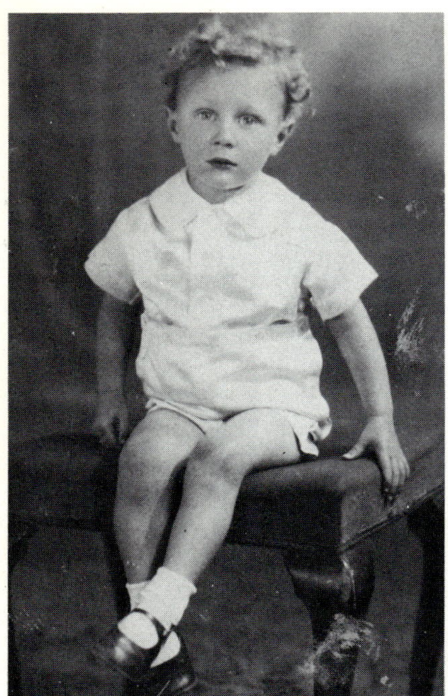

MANCHESTER EVENING NEWS

Above left *A member of Enfield Cricket Club at three years old.*

Above right *Getting the stance right at eleven.*

Below *The North Lancashire Schoolboys team at Old Trafford in 1954. I am the one seated, second from the right. On my right is Alan Bolton, who also played for Lancashire.*

Making my debut for Lancashire in 1968: a championship match against Northamptonshire at Blackpool. Unfortunately, I was soon on my way back, bowled for one by Mushtaq Mohammad.

MANCHESTER EVENING NEWS

MANCHESTER EVENING NEWS

Above *Being welcomed by Lancashire captain, Jack Bond, when I joined the staff at Old Trafford in 1969.*

Below *The Lancashire team in 1974. Back row (from left): John Sullivan, Ken Shuttleworth, Peter Lee, Clive Lloyd, Farokh Engineer, Frank Hayes, Keith Goodwin, and myself; front row: Peter Lever, Ken Snellgrove, David Lloyd (captain), Harry Pilling, David Hughes, and Barry Wood.*

G. HALLAWELL

The Roses clash of 1972 at Old Trafford . . . and two wickets. I finished with 10 for 84 in the match. The top picture shows Richard Hutton being caught by David Lloyd. And below, the finish of the game when I had Chris Clifford lbw in the final over.

PATRICK FAGAR

I am no big hitter like Clive, but have played a few good innings . . .

PATRICK EAGAR

. . . and I have had the privilege to see some great innings from him.

This is agony! Pre-season training for the 1979 season.

More pre-season training — getting in trim for the autograph hunters in cold weather before the 1974 summer.

MANCHESTER EVENING NEWS

of playing the following day so perhaps one or two of us, me included, had a little bit more to drink than was usual on the eve of a big game. Leighton James, the Burnley footballer, came along to wish us all the best and towards the end of the evening, during which we had had our usual pre-match discussions, I knew I had drunk a bit too much. It was the practice before a Gillette match in those days for us to be treated to a free meal and free drinks in a private room, which I always thought was a little bit crackers. Perhaps, though, it wasn't all that potty seeing we weren't likely to drink very much and it wouldn't cost as much as if it had been provided after the game. Smart thinking, I guess. Anyway, I remember going to bed that night and thinking: "Simmo, if we start on time tomorrow, you've probably had a bit too much. Just a teeny bit too much." Any doubts we might have had were put out of our minds first thing on the Saturday morning when a thunderstorm made sure there wouldn't be any play, giving us Saturday and Sunday — which was a beautiful day — to ourselves. Kent, however, had to go to Worcester for a John Player League match, a game they won and which provided vital practice. I used the time to complete my travel arrangements to South Africa with the Wanderers' team, going home to Great Harwood on the Saturday and returning the following evening.

We were able to start on time on the Monday morning on a wicket still feeling the effects of the rain which was of great help to the medium pacers, so I was surprised when we decided to bat after winning the toss. We didn't start too well, Kent bowled and fielded magnificently with three of our wickets falling to run-outs. Their fielding was the highlight of the game, particularly that of Alan Ealham who really put on a show and lived up to his great reputation. He hit the stumps fourteen times with his returns and Clive Lloyd was run out as was Ken Shuttleworth who hurt himself in the process, wrenching his knee. Shuttleworth managed to open the bowling but he was in a good deal of pain and couldn't control the ball, sending down wides and no balls in his one and only over of the innings. We still managed to keep it steady and when we had them 89 for six chasing 119 we thought we had a chance. But we couldn't keep it up and Alan Knott and Bob Woolmer steered them through to a thoroughly deserved win. We had had some good games with Kent and while it is always hard to lose we still went along to their dressing room, drank their champagne and held on to our own twelve bottles until we were back in the hotel.

I stayed in London on the Monday night — which was as well after all the champagne — and flew to South Africa with the Wanderers team the following afternoon. That is without question the greatest team I've ever played with, an exciting side with Brian Close captain, Tony Greig, Glenn Turner, Ian Chappell, Graham McKenzie, Graeme Pollock, John Shepherd, Eddie Barlow, as well as four non-Test players in Peter Sainsbury, Tony Brown, Pasty Harris and me. We didn't lose a game but what pleased me more was bowling in tandem with Sainsbury and proving a highly successful pair in one-day games. Greig urged me on through my nervousness in the first game and I fielded throughout on the boundary edge, an unusual place for me. But there was no way I was going in the slips with a bunch of superstars like that.

By the start of the 1975 season I had had six full years as a Lancashire cricketer and felt myself firmly established in a side that hadn't changed all that much from that first year of the John Player League in 1969. Several of the players, Peter Lever, Ken Shuttleworth, Barry Wood and Frank Hayes, had won Test caps and we also had two other international stars, of course, in Clive Lloyd and Farokh Engineer. We had won the John Player League twice and been four times to Lord's for the final of the Gillette Cup, an honour we were almost beginning to see as a divine right. Whatever happened in any other tournament, we always seemed to produce the goods in the Gillette. And 1975, a golden summer for English cricket with the first World Cup and the beautiful weather, was to prove no exception as we won our way to the final for the fifth time in six seasons.

We received a bye in the first round that year and were drawn at home in the second to Northants, a team we always rated, especially with such players as Mushtaq Mohammad, Roy Virgin, David Steele, Peter Willey, and Sarfraz Nawaz.

They were usually a hard side to beat — but not this time. They chose to bat and lost Virgin and Steele in Lever's opening over, never recovered and were bowled out for 106. The wicket was not easy, that's for sure, and Wood showed just how difficult it was by batting for two and a half hours and 36 overs for 28 not out as we won by nine wickets. Frank Hayes the strokemaker, refused to hang around and hit 56 not out, a fine innings, but not enough to win the gold award which went to Lever for his four for 18 in 12 overs, great bowling that won the match for us.

Hampshire visited Old Trafford in the quarter-final, a formidable side with star players in Barry Richards, Gordon Greenidge and Andy Roberts who helped bring a crowd of over 20,000 to the ground for another game which we won with ridiculous ease and the only full Gillette game in which I didn't bat or bowl. They chose to bat first, as a lot of sides did then, and on a wicket helping the seamers they went from 32 for none to 63 for seven and 98 all out. We wobbled a little bit, and it took Hayes and Engineer to see us through from the uncertain position of 63 for four. Wood had stayed there for a while for 20 runs and that, plus a bowling return of four for 17, gave him a great chance of yet another Man of the Match award. This time, though, it went to one of our new boys, Bob Ratcliffe, who had bowled really well to dismiss Greenidge, Richard Gilliat, Peter Sainsbury and Bob Stephenson for 25 runs. Nobody could have been more excited or delighted and I think all the lads were pleased for him. He was always a nervous type and very excitable so it was specially pleasing to see a match-winning performance by him.

And who should we get in the semi-final, again at Old Trafford, but Gloucestershire! And sure enough there was another 20,000-plus crowd to see a game that was just as exciting as the twilight one four years earlier. They were a fine side with Sadiq Mohammad, Roger Knight, Zaheer Abbas, Mike Procter, David Shepherd, and Tony Brown the captain, so they were never going to be a pushover. Yet somehow, we just couldn't lose to them. It must have driven them frantic at times. Gloucestershire must have thought it was their turn to win after three defeats in five years and they couldn't have asked for a much better start when they batted than an opening century stand. Sadiq had a marvellous innings of 122 but Knight, Zaheer and Procter contributed only 15 between them and really, after such a sound start, they ought to have totalled more than 236. I only bowled three overs for six runs that day and shared my allocation with Clive Lloyd who got the wickets of Sadiq and Procter. I knew there were Gloucester supporters there that day but you'd hardly have known for all the cheering seemed to be for Lancashire, a great feeling as the atmosphere at Old Trafford for a one-day game was always electrifying. Playing at home was worth quite a few runs to us and lifted everybody.

When we replied we were struggling at 182 for six before David Hughes and I put on 39 badly needed runs before I ran him out. We had got behind the scoring rate but that was the way David and I played. It was no use trying to get five or six an over as soon as you went in, you had to take your time, get used to the conditions, have a look at each bowler, and then get going. Procter bowled only seven overs, due to a swollen knee, and this was a real encouragement, for he could have made life uncomfortable for us. He was the type of player who never gave up and I'm sure that he, more than anybody else, wanted to beat Lancashire. It wasn't to be again, although we needed 18 runs off the last 11 balls with Ratcliffe in and the Gloucester lads, I'm certain, feeling they'd got us at last. Jack Davey and Brown bowled those last two overs and we were scrambling about for runs and taking risks as we got closer and closer. I played one magnificent cover drive which got an outside edge and flew past Andy Stovold, the wicketkeeper, to the boundary, one of the easiest positions to get four runs. We got to the last over, from Brown, and with four balls to go, we were one run behind with Ratcliffe on strike. "What do I do?" he asked me. I told him all the fielders would come in to save the singles, so if the ball was there, he had to hit it, either over the top or through the field. I could tell how nervous he was, but I must admit I wasn't feeling on top of the world myself. Nerves didn't show quite so much in me. As senior professional I had to cool him down and make him feel there wasn't too much of a problem! So Brown ran up for the third ball of the last over and Bob laced into it. He was one of the few players at Old Trafford at the time who could really play shots, a bad starter but a good striker of the ball, one who could easily get flustered but once he got a sight of the ball could hit it as well as anybody. Brown's third ball was reasonably well pitched up and Bob laid into it with a full, straight bat and it went past Brown for four. Bob couldn't control himself and came running down the wicket, jumping in the air, waving his bat in excitement. I had to feel sorry for Gloucester having come so close. Again Hughes and Simmons had got runs at a vital time and Gloucester must have been getting sick of the sight of us. But again Procter and Brown were the first in our dressing room to congratulate us and have a glass of champagne, another sad day for them but a great one for us as we had won our way to Lord's for the fifth time in six years. I know I left the dressing room that night quite merry.

Of all our six finals in the 1970s, the 1975 one against Middlesex is the one that made least impression. David Lloyd won the toss and put Middlesex in, which was unusual in those days and produced quite a bit of comment. But it was a good move. The ball was seaming about and we had the first four batsmen out for 64 runs and although Graham Barlow, who was still uncapped then, Larry Gomes and Phil Edmonds got runs, they still only reached 180 for eight. Everybody thought Lancashire were home and dry again but Middlesex had other ideas. Mike Brearley, deciding he had to get wickets if he was going to contain us, bowled out his two best bowlers, Mike Selvey and Fred Titmus, quite early. Only 49 runs came from their 24 overs, but they took only one wicket between them. It did force us to score at about five an over but Clive Lloyd came to our rescue again and hit 73 not out to follow his memorable century in the World Cup final a few weeks earlier. Clive was dropped by Smith early in his innings, very hard but a straightforward chance into the midriff that probably cost Middlesex the game. Brearley had finished with his two best bowlers so that Tim Lamb, Edmonds, who was not as good a bowler then as he is today, Gomes and Featherstone had to see it through. We had wickets in hand and while it probably didn't appear to the cricket connoisseur to be all that difficult, believe me, when you're in the dressing room with your pads on, needing five an over in a Lord's final, it seems far from easy. You are bound to be a bit apprehensive and uncertain. I used to have to go in the toilet, take half a dozen newspapers, three cups of tea and just judge from the reaction of the crowd as to how the game was going. Sometimes, even the chairman, Cedric Rhoades, would be in the cubicle next to me, or wandering up and down and he was just as nervous. Happily, we came through it all more often than not, so neither I nor the chairman ever had a heart attack.

We were also in with a chance of winning the County Championship in 1975. We won the first two of the last three matches and went into the final game at Hove against Sussex knowing that if Leicestershire didn't win and we took all the points from our match we could take the title. We started well enough by bowling out Sussex for 160, but after an opening century partnership we slipped away on a rain-affected pitch — wickets were left uncovered then — and were all out for 222 knowing we had needed 300 for full bonus batting points. Missing those last two bonus points meant we couldn't overhaul Leicestershire who had been struggling in their match. Maybe the knowledge that they were safe helped them relax for they went on to win their game, and the Championship, and leave us, after the Sussex match was washed out, in fourth place. That was to prove the last time for a decade that we were to finish even in the top half of the table. We did have a chance of finishing runners-up to Leicester if we could have beaten Sussex; in their second innings we had them 17 for four, then 120 for six when more rain arrived and washed out the final day. It was disappointing, getting so close after not winning the Championship since 1950, when we shared it with Surrey. Still, it had been a good season, winning the Gillette Cup, reaching the quarter-final of the Benson and Hedges Cup, finishing fourth in the championship and halfway up the John Player League table.

By this time Lancashire supporters used to book their hotels in London for the Gillette Cup final right at the beginning of the season, or even earlier. They were so used to going that they just bought tickets and booked hotels even before the first game had been played. One or two of them must have had second thoughts during our opening game in the 1976 competition when we played Middlesex in a repeat of the previous year's final. They started well, passing 200 with only three wickets down and going on to reach 270 for nine which is a pretty formidable total. The bowler to suffer was yours truly, hit for 89 runs in 12 overs, a number of the runs coming from sixes. When we had discussed the game the previous day David Lloyd had decided in his wisdom that I would bowl my 12 overs at the end of the innings, a policy that didn't prove to be all that successful. I was bowling from the Warwick Road end and every batsman seemed to hit me just where he wanted. We didn't dare let Barry Wood open the batting with so many runs needed and he was dropped right down the order as Farokh Engineer and Andrew Kennedy opened the innings. Farokh only got 12, probably off one over and all on the legside the way he played! But a stand of 101 between Harry Pilling and Frank Hayes gave us real hope and kept the momentum going. I suppose this was one of the greatest features of the Lancashire side then, that we never seemed to panic, if we had wickets in hand we knew we had a better chance of getting the runs. We were 251 for six when I went in, but we were behind the clock with overs running out and Mike Gatting being left to bowl the 58th over. David Hughes and I were together and decided we had to have a go at Gatting who was bowling into the wind. I only scored 17 in that match but they all came in that over from Gatting to leave us needing two from the last two overs. Allan Jones bowled the first of those overs and brought up Edmonds to the bat-pad position. He bowled one short and I just played it down for Edmonds to put out his hand and take the catch. Nobody was worried, least of all me. Wood, batting at nine, hit a single, Hughes got another and we had won by three wickets with eight balls to spare, a really fine win that gave us a lot of satisfaction.

I couldn't believe the quarter-final draw when I heard it — Gloucestershire yet again at Old Trafford. It turned out to be our easiest win of them all, after we put them in and bowled them out for 125 on a wicket taking spin, and on which Hughes took two for 15 and me two for 21, the only bowlers to bowl the full allocation of 12 overs. With our consistent batting this was never going to be a problem. We had an opening stand of 81 between Wood and Engineer before winning by seven wickets with more than 20 overs to spare.

The semi-final was against Warwickshire at Edgbaston where we had lost the Benson and Hedges Cup quarter-final two months earlier. This time we beat them by six wickets after keeping them down to a total of 233 of which Rohan Kanhai scored 49, the top score, before being run out. Kanhai was watching the umpire after Peter Lever had appealed for lbw against him and while he was waiting for the decision, the quick-thinking Wood had collected the ball and run him out. Hayes scored 93 out of 160 in our reply but there was Wood with an innings of 105 to win his third Man of the Match award of the season, his thirteenth in all.

We played in a Lord's final for the sixth time in seven years on 4 September 1976, and never had we been such red-hot favourites as we played Northants, a county that had never won anything in 100 years and were in a final for the first time. The pitch looked a little green and I thought that winning the toss would provide an advantage. Northants won it, put us in and in no time we were not only 45 for three with Engineer, Pilling and Hayes out, but we had also lost Wood, hit on the finger by a ball from John Dye and forced to retire to take no further part in the game. It was a funny thing about Engineer who always enjoyed the atmosphere of the big occasion yet never really got any runs at Lord's. His wicketkeeping, however, was always of the highest class and in my eyes he was the best I've ever seen. We did manage to pull round with David Lloyd, David Hughes and John Abrahams, playing in his first Lord's final, giving us some respectability at 195 for seven. What did surprise us was that Dye, who bowled seven overs for nine runs and took Engineer's wicket, didn't return to the attack. Instead, Bishen Bedi, the left-arm spinner, was preferred. We were in deep trouble going into the last over at 169 for seven and we were all taken by surprise when Bedi was kept on for the final over against

Hughes, one of the best strikers of the ball in the country, particularly against spinners. He keeps his eye on the ball and gives it an almighty whack with superb timing. This day he hit 26 runs in that final over, including two great sixes to the sight-screen at the Nursery End — pretty big hits. Bedi finished with three for 52 in 11 overs and with 26 coming off that last over it shows just how well he must have bowled earlier. And to show what sort of person he is, each time Hughes hit him for six, he still had the grace and sportsmanship to applaud him. Getting closer to 200 at least gave us something to bowl at but we didn't begin well and Roy Virgin and Peter Willey got away to a start of 103 which made it look all over bar the shouting. But Lancashire sides never gave up in those days and they continued trying to save the game and I must say I finished up proud of that performance, except for the result. Northants were 103 for none but finished 199 for six and were taken to the 59th over before they won. We made them fight every inch of the way which pleased everybody and we were handicapped by Wood not being able to bowl and field in what turned out to be our last Gillette Cup final ever. I don't think our chairman, Cedric Rhoades, regarded 1976 as being too good as we finished sixteenth in the Championship after being fourth the previous year, ninth in the John Player League and knocked out of the Benson and Hedges Cup at the quarter-final stage. A trophy, I suppose, is what makes a successful season.

That season turned out to be the last for Engineer, Shuttleworth and Sullivan, three stalwarts of the Lancashire side through the great years, and it was then that I felt that the team I had grown with from my first season in 1969 was starting to break up. It it always sad to see players leave, especially players you have shared so many happy and successful years with and I really did feel that Engineer, in particular, left too early. He was still a fine wicketkeeper and though he was thirty-eight and he left Lancashire at his own request, I still think he could have given us useful service.

7
TROUBLE IN THE CAMP

It would be wrong of me to give the impression that all was wine and roses at Lancashire through the years we were having so much success, reaching six Gillette Cup finals in the seven years from 1970 to 1976. There was a problem within the dressing room, stemming a good deal from money, but also from principles we felt had to be upheld. Troubles came to a head in 1975, a great summer in so many ways in England with the beautiful weather, the visit of the Australians, and the first-ever World Cup which was such a success and which was won by the West Indies. Any problems we had at Lancashire had usually been ironed out before the season started, but this year nothing had been decided, particularly with regard to our salary and what it would be for the season. The matter had drifted on to the end of May when we went to Northampton for a championship match, a game we won by 201 runs and from where we issued a statement which I read over the phone to the then secretary, to the effect that if the matter wasn't dealt with by the time we got to the next match at Buxton, the problem would become serious. He asked if all the players, including Clive Lloyd who was with us before leaving to join the West Indies for the World Cup, felt like this. I said Clive was in agreement; he said he didn't believe Clive would support us so I had to put Clive on the telephone to convince him. The secretary suggested another meeting but I said the players wouldn't agree to that because they were fed up of being stalled. He rang back to suggest a meeting at Buxton on the eve of the match with Derbyshire so we met in one of the hotel rooms. David Lloyd, our captain, sat alongside the secretary at the meeting and didn't appear to be on the players' side because he thought it would all be sorted out by the chairman. The secretary, who didn't seem to have notified the chairman and the committee of the players' unrest, assured us that things would be dealt with immediately and so we played at Buxton.

That game, incidentally, turned out to be one of the most amazing I have ever played in, Lancashire winning by an innings and 348 runs in a game affected by snow! The first day, a Saturday, was lovely and we scored 477 for five in the 100 overs we were allowed, with centuries from Clive Lloyd and Frank Hayes. When I went in to bat we were 306 for five and Clive was still there, close to 50. By the time he got to 100, I was 45 so I had done pretty well to keep up with him. But by the time we finished our innings around six o'clock I had gone from 45 to only 55 while Clive had moved from 100 to 167 as he hit six after six, with balls landing on the bowling green and poor old Fred Swarbrook being hit for 111 runs in 17 overs. Soon after Clive had reached 100, Dusty Rhodes, one of the umpires, moved back three or four yards from the stumps. I asked him where he was going. "This fellow is hitting straight and very hard and I would like to have more room to manoeuvre," he said. "But what about no balls?" I asked. And Dusty replied: "I don't think this fellow is going to be too bothered about no balls."

The same thing had happened against Warwickshire in 1971 when Clive scored a double century. Being at the other end was like being in a firing range. Dusty Rhodes was umpire then, too, and he did exactly the same thing. Clive has hit a few umpires with his driving and I can recall Dickie Bird, Jack Van Geloven and Rhodes, who was always extremely wary after that Warwickshire experience as it was quite frightening to be at the other end when Clive was in that mood. When you are backing up, the distance from Clive is nearer fifteen yards than twenty-two and the ball is travelling faster than any bowler can deliver it, easily 100 miles an hour which doesn't give you much time to get out of the way.

He hit eight sixes in his innings at Buxton, his last 67 runs coming in 37 minutes as Lancashire reached a total never before achieved in 100 overs. By the end of the day Derbyshire were 25 for two and still had to score another 303 runs to avoid following-on. I know we had worked it out that if we bowled tidily through the 100 overs — innings were suspended after 100 in those days — we could still make them follow-on! We went to Colchester on the Sunday where we lost a John Player League match and were late getting back to Buxton that night. I was sharing a room with David Hughes with a window overlooking the main street and we weren't fully awake on the Monday morning when a foreign waiter arrived with our morning tea. The curtains were drawn so I casually asked what the weather was like. In broken English he replied: "It's snowing." As it was 2 June, I thought to myself: "The fool, he doesn't know what I'm saying." I pulled the curtain and looked up at a clear blue sky. Then I pulled it back properly and saw snow on the ground. I was astonished. At breakfast we were told we wouldn't start on time but lunch would be served at the ground and there would be an inspection about midday. We were in the dressing room about noon waiting to see when we could start as the ground dried under the hot sun when it started to go dark. The clouds closed in and the first flakes of snow began to fall soon after. That was astonishing enough at the beginning of June but what followed was amazing. The day grew blacker and for twenty minutes we were hit by the worst snow storm I have ever seen. I couldn't see the other side of the ground or the surrounding houses until the clouds lifted to leave a beautiful winter's picture. Clive Lloyd was seeing snow for only the third time in his life and he was dashing about looking for a photographer to capture the happy scene. The sun was soon shining again and as the snow melted the steam rose as if the ground were a huge cauldron. We thought that not only would we not be able to play that day but we would also be denied our chance of winning the following day as well.

But on the Tuesday it was beautiful again and the game started on time to produce an astonishing day's cricket. Wickets were uncovered then and while the pitch was soft the surrounds were all right. We hadn't a clue how the snow-affected pitch would play but we were soon to find out as wickets tumbled in quick succession to give us victory by three o'clock. Derbyshire went from Saturday's 25 for two to 42 all out in their first innings and followed-on 435 behind to be bowled out again, this time for 87, to give Lancashire one of the biggest wins they had ever had. Obviously we were pleased, but we knew as well as anybody that we couldn't consider it a fair win. In fact, we were glad to come away without seriously injuring anybody. We were really frightened for the opposition for the only time I can remember. They weren't all that keen on batting on such a pitch either and a few of the batsmen who hit balls in the air were heard to plead: "Please catch it." There was one amusing incident when Ashley Harvey-Walker was batting. After the first ball had shot past his nose as he played forward, he went over to umpire Dickie Bird at square leg and handed him his false teeth, wrapped in his handkerchief. Soon after, he fended off a ball from Peter Lee and as he turned away, he didn't see David Lloyd catch it and pocket it. Harvey-Walker looked round then said to Lloyd: "Did you catch it?" Lloyd said he had. "Thank Heaven for that," said Harvey-Walker who collected his false teeth from Dickie as he left the field.

Lancashire lost five players to the World Cup after that match, Peter Lever, Frank Hayes and Barry Wood to England, Clive Lloyd to the West Indies and Farokh Engineer to the Indian team. The rest of us went off to firstly Ilford where I was able to bat at number five and scored 96 not out against Essex before the overs ran out. It didn't make any difference, as I still slid down the order a couple of places for the next match against Cambridge.

We had been assured our problems at Old Trafford would be sorted out and that is where our next game was played, against Middlesex, a match we won by eight wickets with only one of our World Cup players, Engineer, back in the side. That game started on a Wednesday — 18 June — the same day that England were losing to Australia in the World Cup semi-final at Headingley. Only one of our England players came to the ground the following day and the other two left it until Friday before they arrived, an attitude that disappointed the rest of us. We discussed the matter, but not thoroughly, in the two days we had and while we were ready to take action we didn't want to break our contracts. Most players invariably carry injuries and we had thought we would all drop out through injury.

At this time we were high in the Championship table, having won four games before the middle of June so we naturally fancied our chances of beating Derbyshire in the next match at Old Trafford, starting the following day, Saturday, 21 June. But on the Saturday morning, shortly before we were due to start the match, the place was in turmoil as the three England players, Lever, Hayes and Wood, said they wouldn't play. The rest of us felt it wouldn't do any good because the chairman, Cedric Rhoades, was in London attending the World Cup final. But the three said they were going ahead anyway and words between the players were getting heated in the dressing room as the time approached for the match to start. Eventually Lever, Wood, and Hayes said they would not play because they were injured. Harry Pilling and I had genuine injuries — Pilling's legs were black and blue. We were both having treatment when David Lloyd came to ask if we were injured or if we were playing. Pilling said: "Am I picked? If I'm picked, I'll play," and I decided the same. So in the end Lancashire went into the match with only the three England players missing while others had to be quickly drafted into the side, including Bob Ratcliffe who was shopping at home in Accrington before going to a League club as their professional in the afternoon. The flak soon started flying, of course, and members could be heard asking what was happening. The three players were told they had to have medicals but Wood refused and after an emergency committee meeting all three were disciplined, Lever and Hayes being dropped for two matches, Wood for six. David Hughes and I seemed to spend almost the whole of the next two days on the phone to the Players Association and the chairman and other people trying to sort the matter out to the best conclusion.

We were disappointed at the attitude of our England players who seemed to feel that as Test cricketers in a county team they could have a more important voice in matters because they had the extra confidence in knowing they wouldn't be sacked. The rest of us were expected to follow them like lambs. We didn't want to stop the game but they were adamant over their decision, regardless of us. Afterwards, they felt we had let them down, and we felt they had let us down. The problem was soon sorted out to our satisfaction. Even now, I still think the three players were wrong. But maybe if I'd been an England player I'd have done exactly the same and got annoyed with people who wouldn't fight for rights, but expected the benefits.

8
CRICKET ALL THE YEAR ROUND

I was in only my second full year in county cricket, when Dickie Bird, the umpire, who spent his winters as head coach in Johannesburg, asked me if I would like to join him coaching in South Africa. Why he asked me, a new boy, I don't know. Whether he thought I was the sort of person to do a job without too much hassle over pay and conditions I'm not quite sure. That was 1970 and I turned him down mainly because I was a bit afraid of the insecurity of giving up my job in the winter and going abroad. I had become a qualified draughtsman working at the Lancashire County Surveyor's department in Bamber Bridge, near Preston, and I enjoyed it. The promotion and the increments were there, the prospects of furthering my career were far better than they had ever been at Accrington Brick and Tile Company so to give that up for the insecurity of being a cricketer for twelve months of the year didn't appeal to me.

Dickie asked me again in 1971 so I talked it over with my wife, Jacqueline, who said I seemed to be secure with Lancashire, who were doing pretty well at the time, and perhaps going to South Africa wouldn't be the great risk that we thought. I went to see the County Surveyor, whose love of cricket had persuaded him to release me for six months of the year but still let me have my position back every September and allow me increments each year over six months instead of twelve. However, he said he couldn't guarantee my job back if things didn't go well and I didn't like coaching in South Africa. So it was a gamble. It was Jacqueline who really made up my mind for me in the end and pointed out that we would be able to see parts of the world we had never seen before. So after the English cricket season of 1971 we went to Johannesburg where Dickie was head coach with several other county players, Clive Radley (Middlesex), Kevin Lyons (Glamorgan), Alan Gordon (Warwickshire), Bob Woolmer (Kent) and Peter Stringer (Yorkshire), although the last two were at private schools and not with Transvaal Cricket Union. It really was a big adventure for us. All right, I had to pay for Jacqueline to go and the money wasn't that good, but the excitement and enjoyment of seeing other parts of the world was tremendous. We stayed at an hotel called the Jacaranda in Hill Brow, one of the heaviest populated communities in the world, we were told. We enjoyed the hotel and lived there for some time but we were only getting 250 rand, about £125 a month, so to make it easier on our salaries Clive, Kevin, Alan, Jacqueline and I rented a house in a very nice area, Lock Avenue, which had three bedrooms. Jacqueline became cook, bottle washer, cleaner, laundry woman, the lot, as well as taking a job in a departmental store to help us eventually break even. And as she was doing the work for everybody the rent was divided by four, instead of five, which also helped us through.

I was eager to impress in my new job and was asked after a few weeks if I would play for East Rand Premier Mine (E.R.P.M.) on Sundays, one of the deepest mines in South Africa, which paid me fifteen rand, about £7.50, a game. I was also playing in the Northern Transvaal League which included Geoff Boycott and Pat Pocock, and thoroughly enjoyed it. I had a fantastic season, failing to get five wickets in an innings only twice, I think, and getting runs quite regularly as well. We didn't win the League but finished in the top three, which was higher than they had been for some years, and reached the final of the knockout cup. The players were tremendously keen with Dougie Holmes, the captain, and his brother having a great influence on the success of the club. I was only there a year but we still keep in touch, fifteen years on. Overseas players were not allowed to play in the Saturday league then but we were made complimentary members of the great Wanderers' club which must be one of the best in the world. There were three cricket ovals with the main one being the old Test ground, squash, golf, exercise centres and restaurants, an Olympic pool and most of our Saturdays were taken up there. The best tan I ever got was during that stay in South Africa. The salary Northern Transvaal paid was insufficient to live on. But they knew this and helped subsidise the wage by organising coaching clinics in various areas over the long Christmas holiday period.

Dickie stayed at a private school, a sideline for him, where he coached their first team and went to Saturday matches with them. Dickie had always been a bachelor and he loved to come round to our house and sample Jacqueline's cooking which would earn him some ribbing from the others who would tell him: "You can't come in here and have a meal, Dickie, you're not contributing towards it." Sometimes after nets we'd go back for lunch where Jacqueline had left me something to eat and I'd split it with him — which isn't something I do regularly. As soon as the others came in Dickie would say: "Jack invited me, Jack invited me!" Schools didn't allow cricket coaching to take precedence over school work so most schools finished about two o'clock or halfpast which is when you found the keen ones staying behind to be coached. Our mornings were spent at the Wanderers' club swimming, exercising, playing squash, or having nets which is where Dickie, more than any one at that time, really helped me. When we were at Heathrow on our way to South Africa, I had asked Dickie why he hadn't given me any lbw decisions in the three years I had been playing. He agreed he hadn't and said it was quite simple — I had been bowling far too wide of the return crease. Therefore if a batsman was on the front foot and the ball turned it was going to miss leg stump. "Even if it doesn't turn, which you don't do too much of anyway," he added, "it will probably still miss leg stump or be outside the line of off stump, so I can't give him out." So Dickie helped me get closer to the stumps when I bowled. I practised at the other lads who were with us, got closer and closer to the stumps, until Dickie announced one day: "Fine, now your foot is dropping in the batsman's mark and you're landing round about middle stump so that's making you bowl between wicket and wicket. Now, if you get somebody on the front foot and the ball hits low on the pad and it's about middle and off, it has every chance of carrying on and hitting the wickets." I was very pleased with myself because it had been hard work but I was getting better and better.

One of the perks about going to Johannesburg was being able to cruise back home on the Reina del Mar which took fourteen days and gave you a break from cricket, allowed you to relax and revitalise ready for the new season. We were in the bar one night and I cornered Dickie and asked him: "With all the hard work I've been doing and help you've given me, if I bowl where I've been bowling in South Africa, I must have a chance of getting lbw decisions." Dickie agreed.

I was soon back at Old Trafford, in the first team again and fit as a flea. And who should be officiating at one of our early games but Harold Dennis Bird who came towards me as we walked out to field and asked if I'd seen the wicket. "I think it'll turn, Jack, but not at my end." Anyway when I was put on to bowl, it was at Dickie's end and after a couple of overs I hit the batsman — I forget who — on the pad, not on the front foot, but on the back and it was one of those occasions when I just knew it was out. With Dickie's help in South Africa I had got close to the stumps, the ball was delivered between wicket and wicket, the batsman was back on middle and off and had been hit about six inches above the ankle. I turned to Dickie with a big smile across my face and said: "How's that one, Harold Dennis?" And he said: "Not out, Jack, not out." I told him he had to be joking, I had fulfilled all his requirements, the batsman was even on the back foot. There was no way he could not be out. Dickie said: "Jack, you've done everything right, got close to the stumps, bowled between wicket and wicket, but you've got so close to the stumps and gone so much in front of me I couldn't even see the batsman. So it's not out!" I thought he was taking the mickey, perhaps making an excuse so he didn't have to give me the decision, but I found out from one or two other umpires that I was getting in their way, getting my right shoulder over and shielding the flight of the ball, so I had to go back to the drawing board and get that bit further away from the stumps or pivot on my front foot. Since then I've had many decisions off Dickie. We've always been good friends and been able to talk together and he's the man who made me work hard on this part of my game. Otherwise I would have missed a lot of lbw decisions in my career.

That season in South Africa gave me a real bug for coaching and the success I had as a player meant I had no problems being invited back by E.R.P.M. on a better salary and also as a coach with Transvaal Cricket Union. So Jacqueline and myself were looking forward through the English summer of 1972 to returning to South Africa in the winter. But though we didn't know it, Tasmania was just around the corner . . .

9
A VIP IN TASMANIA

While I was in my fourth season with Lancashire — in 1972 — the club chairman, Cedric Rhoades, asked me if I had any employment for that coming winter. I had been asked to go back to South Africa as coach and player and had agreed without signing anything. The chairman asked if I would like to go to Tasmania, a place I knew about only through Peter Lever who had been coaching there the previous winter after touring Australia in 1970–71 with Ray Illingworth's team. The chairman said Peter wouldn't be going back as there had been a little bit of friction and if I wanted to go I should write to Tom Room who was chairman of the Northern Tasmania Cricket Association. I thought it would be a nice change to go to the Australian island instead of South Africa and knowing what Peter had been paid, I knew that sort of money would make it easier for Jacqueline. About a month later Mr Rhoades said Tom Room had been in touch with him to say I was on the short list of three. He didn't know anything about me but would take the chairman's word on me as a person, on my character and temperament. The chairman suggested I ring Mr Room and we seemed to hit it off straight away on the phone. The job was mine and the contract arrived soon after with an offer that was far above anything I had anticipated and was three or four times better than what I had received in South Africa.

Jacqueline and I flew direct to Tasmania at the beginning of October, 1972, and what a reception was waiting for us at Launceston. I'd never known anything like this. After all it wasn't as if Clive Lloyd was arriving, I was just a bread and butter county player. Launceston airport is beautiful and small, and as we walked across the tarmac I could see several people coming towards the plane, one with a TV camera, photographers among them. I said there must be somebody famous or important on the plane. But there was nobody else getting off. It was for us! We were ushered into the VIP lounge in the airport for photographs and interviews and I was taken aback by all this superstar welcome. What surprised me more was the question about what I intended doing. I had assumed that seeing the Northern Tasmania Cricket Association had flown me 12,000 miles, supplied me with a flat and a car as well as paying me a reasonable salary, that they would be telling me what they wanted. It was only later that I found the importance they attached to professional English cricketers going out there to coach. Peter Lever, David Evans, Alan Knott and Neil Hawke, the Australian Test player, had all been there before me which was a measure of the importance they put on us to lift the playing standard and to coach. One of the best schemes I had ever seen had been in South Africa where the basics of cricket were taught at primary level and interest was maintained by going round the schools and organising competitions for youngsters during school holidays. Tasmania already had under-16 and under-18 teams but there was no way cricket and enthusiasm could be maintained if club sides did not have facilities and competitions for youngsters aged between twelve and fifteen. I started by involving the six clubs that made up the Northern Tasmania Cricket Association and went round the schools, coaching at thirty-two primaries in Launceston and the northern area. I felt nervous at the schools where teachers and some parents wanted to be involved and became even more nervous when a TV crew was sent round to televise a coaching programme.

Each of the six N.T.C.A. clubs were allocated the coach in turn each season and I was sent to South Launceston, one of the two clubs that had so far not had a coach. We made good friends there, particularly with the Donaldsons, four lads and parents Marie and Alan who were like second parents to Jacqueline and myself. When I first went to the club to practise I was amazed at the number of people there, over 100 between the two clubs who were using the four nets, only about seven in each net but everybody else so enthusiastic that there were little groups of slip catchers, high catchers and the others exercising and running round the ground. It was wonderful to see but quite a surprise and a change from what you find in most League cricket clubs in England. There were only under-16 teams in junior cricket which was something I started to change and one of the early schools I remember visiting was West Launceston where one of the teachers, Peter Jones, became a good friend. I know he was keen, but was wary of English coaches, wondering whether the schools would get value for money. He gave a lot of time to the under-13 team and he watched me go through the grip, the stance, the back lift, the various shots. A lesson I quickly learned was that it was important to keep youngsters interested, ensure that they enjoyed it. So I have always taught a youngster how to hit a ball, they enjoy that best and that is what they will remember, and I mix that with the boring bits in the hope they won't forget either. And I always teach them the hook shot, though I had never called it that, at least, I never pronounced it properly. From my early days, probably coming from the brickyard and the Enfield club, I had always called it the "'ooook' shot." When I announced to twenty-four youngsters that we would play the "'ooook' shot," they all stood aghast as if I was a foreigner — which I suppose I was — and they couldn't understand a word. I didn't know what was the matter so I continued: "Now when do you play the 'ooook' shot?" There was no answer so I said: "Surely, you know when to play the 'ooook' shot." And one youngster said: "What is the 'ooook' shot?" They simply couldn't understand me so I asked what they called it and was told the "hook shot" as in book. In those days I probably said "booook" as well but I knew what they were saying and I learned to say hook in the more understandable way. So I learned quickly to speak better, not to chop off words before they are completed as the Lancashire accent does from time to time, and to be more careful in my speech. It might have helped me out there but when I returned to the Old Trafford dressing room the following season, Harry Pilling said to me: "You've got bloody posh, haven't you?"

I thoroughly enjoyed going to the schools, mostly primary, going as far as Westbury in the north, to Campbell Town in the Midlands, Avoca on the east and occasionally up to Devonport usually after the Christmas period. There was quite a bit of driving to do but a car and sponsorship were provided and everything was generally well organised. Usually when I arrived at the schools the kids were ready in white shorts and white tee-shirts, something Peter Lever got going. He set a good example and they were keen. It took until my third season to really get the under-13s going, involving teachers and clubs, and I was pleased to see Tom Room buy a nice trophy competed for in the Jack Simmons Under-13s week, an event I am happy to say is still held. When I was young I always wanted to play at Old Trafford, the Mecca of cricket for me, and I assumed Tasmanian youngsters wanted the same, to play on the N.T.C.A. ground at Launceston. So we started this in my first year, got clubs involved with trials, parents brought the youngsters and also became interested, and I thought it was the right ladder for young boys to start on.

Clubs didn't have bars or social clubs as they do now. Every dressing room had its own bar, cans of beer were brought in and paid for and profits went to club funds. There were hamburgers and steaks and sausages — all with tomato sauce — and the fridge was full of beer. I've never turned my nose up at food and drink and immediately the game was over we would get a cold can of beer and sit and chat about the game for hours! We could finish the game at six or six-thirty and the lads would still be there at ten. Wives and girl friends weren't allowed in the dressing rooms and would still be waiting outside in the cars. Now Jacqueline would allow me a lot of my own way but wouldn't go so far as waiting four hours for me. So she soon decided I'd been there long enough and set off for the dressing room. "Where are you going?" the girls asked. "I'm going to knock on the door," she said. "If he isn't ready, I'm off. He'll have to get a lift." The girls said she couldn't do that, but they didn't know Jacqueline. She could, and a few other wives started doing the same thing. So I suppose she could be said to have liberated some of the womenfolk in Launceston. As time went on women and children were invited in after the players had showered and changed and now they have a social club which I plugged for from the first year, a great success.

The first game I played for South Launceston was at Campbell Town against the Midlands side, forty miles south of Launceston on the way to Hobart, on a ground that was as big, if not bigger than, Old Trafford. It was the start of the cricket season and they still had the goalposts up from the Aussie Rules football in the winter. It was the first game in early October and was windy and not that warm. The ground only had three cricket strips which were played on all season, going from one to another as they recovered much more quickly than those in England. I found I wasn't making too much of a footmark on the tarry black soil which could get just a bit sticky when wet, so curators didn't have to be re-turfing footholds as we have to do many times in England. The pitch looked greenish and I didn't think it would turn much so decided to open the bowling with medium pace or what I thought was quick. I asked the captain if he minded if I bowled a few seamers and he agreed. They had never seen me at the nets because I had only arrived a few days earlier. Naturally I was out to impress and I roared in as fast as I could — I was a bit more supple in those days — and let fly with an outswinger which beat the bat and hit Nevin Donaldson, the wicket-keeper, in the chest before he had the chance to get his gloves to it. He picked up the ball and said: "So you're only a medium pacer? That's quick here for our side." So I fairly impressed them but tired quickly. I bowled half a dozen overs, got two wickets, bowled a few spinners and got a couple more, then finished off the tail bowling quick again and ended with six for 57. They were bowled out for 146 so both the club and myself were happy, a good foot to start on.

I had started well and continued in the same vein. The wickets were a bit more difficult to bowl on than in England but as I got used to them I picked up more wickets in the second half of the season. I enjoyed batting on those wickets and my highest ever score came in a game against Mowbray who had one of the best attacks, including Peter Warren who had played state cricket. The games were over two weekends and Mowbray had scored 253 for seven declared. We quickly lost both openers and at tea I was 43 not out and we needed something over 150 more to win in about two hours. Our lads thought we might draw but I scored 127 more after tea and it was probably one of the best knocks I've ever played as we went on to win. I was quite pleased as I didn't think I had the patience or concentration to score 170. I had arrived in early October and by late November I had got the highest score of my life. The following day, in the N.T.C.A. knockout competition, I got 84 not out in the win over Launceston so in two knocks I had scored 254 not out, a great weekend for Jack Simmons and, of course, for South Launceston.

When I first went to Tasmania the only first-class game they played was against the country touring Australia at the time. They also played in the Gillette Cup, just one game as they always got knocked out at the start. The team for the Gillette match was selected over what they called the long weekend with one-day games on the Saturday, Sunday and Monday, involving the three Associations from the south, the north and north-west of Tasmania, with the north-west being considerably weaker than the other two. I was captain of the north and on the Saturday we beat the south as I took two wickets, scored runs and ran one of their best players out. Tony Benneworth, one of the senior and best players in the north, came to me after the run-out and asked what I did for an encore. We also beat the north-west convincingly on the Monday and we were in the dressing room when Brucie Johns, an old player, came to me and said: "Well played. Two convincing wins. How many players do you think you'll get in the state side from the north?" It was the first chance I'd had of seeing what talent there was throughout the island but, picking from those games, I got what I thought was a pretty good side with eight from the north in the twelve I'd chosen. He had a look at my team, said he could understand my choice, but would I have a bet with him, that there wouldn't be five in the team. I thought I was stealing his money. The team was chosen that night and I was thrilled when I was named as captain ahead of Rodney Cass, the Worcestershire player who coached in the south and had been there the previous year as well. The north had four players in the twelve so I had lost my two-dollar bet. But I found it hard to believe so I went to our selector from the north who told me that from time to time agreement was made between two of the three selectors to get chosen players into the side and a 2-1 vote meant they got what they wanted. Our selector was outvoted on a couple of players so we had four, the north-west had two and the south six.

One of the players was an opening batsman called Brian Cartledge who impressed people with his hitting right from the start. In our game he had hit two fours in the first over and about fifth ball had been bowled. I didn't give him a chance because I thought he was just a slogger. It transpired that about five years earlier he had played for the State against Western Australia, had scored 50 and had hit Tony Lock and one or two others over pine trees, quite some height and distance. But he'd been playing on that one performance for five years. Naturally, as a new boy, I couldn't say much. I couldn't say the selection was absolutely diabolical. One of our players, Gary Knight, scored two 50s in those weekend games and was in the twelve, but on the way to Brisbane for the Gillette Cup match with Queensland about a week later, I was told by the travelling selector that Knight would be twelfth man, regardless of conditions. I said it was ridiculous to leave out the outstanding player of our triangular tournament and I had a long chat with the selector, who had been a Tasmanian player, making him promise that politics would not enter into selection, at least not if they wanted to get into the Sheffield Shield competition and play first-class cricket. It had been drilled into me that that had been their aim for five or six years and I told the N.T.C.A. they would never get into the Sheffield Shield if they chose a team that way. The Tasmanian selectors had certainly got it wrong for this match for, as well as the opening bat who'd had one 50, there were others who hadn't impressed me including a left-arm quickie, built like a brick chicken hut who was good but maybe not good enough. Another promise I got out of the selector on the way to Brisbane was that the captain would be consulted about the twelfth man and a decision made on the morning of the match. It seems they hadn't felt captains in the past had wanted the responsibility of making a selection. That selector resigned the following year and took up flat green bowling so I had wasted time and effort on him.

We practised in the afternoon when we got to Brisbane and had just finished when one of the biggest cloudbursts I have ever seen hit the city and within minutes the ground was awash. I don't think you could see twenty square feet of ground anywhere that wasn't covered with water, washing over the steps to the dressing room, and I thought we wouldn't be able to play the next day. The following morning the selector, plus Rodney Cass, who was vice-captain, Clem Jones, Lord Mayor of Brisbane who was also the curator of the Gabba ground, and myself went onto the ground. It was damp and we couldn't see a prepared pitch anywhere . . . "Anywhere between here and there," said Clem, which covered about twelve yards. Somebody said he hoped he ran the city better than the cricket ground. I won the toss, put them in, and we had them 56 for six going into lunch and the wicket getting easier. During a good stand between Dudgeon and Hohns I chased a ball towards the mid-wicket boundary and stopped it about a yard from the edge. I flicked the ball back with my foot but continued running into the advertising boards and made a great clatter. I threw the ball in and saw the umpire signalling four. I told him it hadn't gone for four but he said it had, he'd heard a noise. I said: "If something like fourteen and a half stone runs into a tin hoarding you're sure to hear a noise. But the ball didn't hit the line." He said he had signalled four and that was the end of it. I said I was sorry, I begged to differ. If it had been a four-day game I wouldn't have minded so much but it could be vital and was unfair in a one-day match. I knew all the states considered Tasmania the Cinderella state, a walkover but I was now beginning to think the umpires thought the same way. He said I would have to abide by his decision and I said I wasn't going to. He walked back to his position behind the stumps but I refused to allow our bowler to bowl. I hadn't lost my temper, but it was about to go and the square leg umpire came across and wanted to know what was happening. I explained and he agreed, saying he knew it hadn't gone for four. He had a word with the other umpire and told him he would have to change his decision and turn it into three runs instead of four. Queensland scrambled past 100 and the excitement on the faces of the Tasmanian lads was amazing as they had never before won a game. Not that we were to win that one as we slid to around 60 for five by the time I went in and joined Cass. He was batting well and I thought if we could get just about 20 runs each that would secure it. I had got a few runs when Cass hit one to cover and called me for a run. I played hell with him as we passed but the wicketkeeper hadn't time to get to the stumps and it was Sam Trimble, fielding at short leg who waited for the return which flew off his arms to fine leg. He had taken the bails off, though, with his hands and when he appealed the umpire gave me out. It was the same umpire I had argued with. Cass came running down the wicket accusing him of cheating but it didn't make any difference and we lost by a few runs.

Tasmania's other game that season was against the tourists, Pakistan, although the island's side then was called a Combined XI as it was reinforced by two players from the mainland who were doing well in the Sheffield Shield and were on the fringe of the Test team. The two given to me were Max Walker and Gary Gilmour. I'd never heard of them but I had to have them in the side whether I wanted to or not and when you are playing as good a batting side as Pakistan you had to be pleased about being given two bowlers. I liked Walker straight away, but Gilmour took longer to get used to. It didn't help, I suppose, him having left his boots in Sydney and arriving at the ground without any, giving the impression that having done well for New South Wales it was a drop in class for him to play for Tasmania, even though he was facing the touring side. Gilmour played in sand shoes — his boots arrived the following day — and started well, swinging the ball after asking to change ends. Walker would have bowled all day, but I don't think Gilmour would. Walker came from Tasmania and knew it was a good chance for him and bowled well after taking the first wicket. I've been a good friend since then of Walker. I liked what I saw, liked his outlook on cricket and the way he put everything into it. Gilmour tried but wasn't as well organised and went out of the game quicker than Walker. The difference in the character of those two players was shown in that game and I was pleased to see Walker get six wickets in the last Test at Sydney. Gilmour might have had more talent but he didn't give me the impression he would have given everything when the going got hard — not the way Walker did. I scored 77 in my first representative match for Tasmania against Pakistan, and got the runs in 53 minutes as I shared in a partnership of 82 with Les Appleton, of which he scored five. Somebody wrote of that innings: "Simmons hooked, slashed and cut in style, reminiscent of Keith Miller at his best." I'm not going to tell you I survived dropped catches when I was 60 and 71.

Everything seemed to fall into place that first season. The coaching was going well, junior cricket was progressing, I was playing well for my club, South Launceston, and had started well for Tasmania. I must say it pleased me no end when the N.T.C.A. asked me if I would return for the 1973–74 season. As I was a paid employee I was surprised when they threw a farewell party for me at the end of my first season. The following year I was allocated to Riverside club, the only one of the N.T.C.A.'s six clubs not to have had the Association coach in their team. They were a good side and we were unbeaten that year, topping the league table by several points and winning the knockout competition, not that I was allowed to play in the finals. After Neil Hawke had had a marvellous all-round performance in his year as coach six years earlier, it was decided not to allow the coach to play in the finals. This was not so in the knockout games in my first year when I was allowed to play and South Launceston won through to the final which we lost to Mowbray. I couldn't play for Riverside though when they won, nor in 1974–75 when they lost, and it always aggrieved me, having to miss out on the closing stages after working hard to get your club side to the top of the ladder. A teammate at Riverside before he left to join Carlton in Melbourne was Tony Benneworth, one of the best Tasmanian players I have ever seen. He was a talented cricketer who didn't like to lose but who didn't perhaps believe enough in his own ability.

After losing to Queensland in my first year in the Gillette

Cup, Tasmania lost to New Zealand in the second year, then drew to play Victoria in the third year, 1974–75, the year England were touring Australia under Mike Denness's captaincy. Victoria were a good side with players like Max Walker, Froggie Thomson, Ray Bright, and Ian Redpath. Our three selectors had chosen twelve players again and again I was told about the twelfth man the day before the match. The odd player out was to be Graham Mansfield, a good all-rounder in form, while a batsman called Jim Wilkinson, who had had a run of three or four "ducks," was in the side. Jim was a good one-day player who liked to get on with it but was out of form, had no confidence and had even got a "duck" in the trial game. I told the travelling selector who was manager that I thought we were making a mistake. He said the other selectors were coming over the following morning and if I thought Mansfield should play he would put it to them. "It's never been done before," he said. After we had had nets the following morning I was on my way back to the dressing room when I was met halfway by the selectors who said they understood I wanted to change the twelfth man. I said I felt it was better for the side, and better for Jim Wilkinson who, I thought, would be very relieved at hearing he wasn't playing. So they said: "All right. If you take full responsibility you can change it."

Ian Redpath won the toss for Victoria and batted first, probably assuming that Victoria would be able to bat us way out of the game. Yet they only reached 190 for seven which put victory within our reach if we just had the confidence in ourselves. We couldn't have had a better start with a partnership of 108 between Sadiq Mohammad, our other overseas player who was playing and coaching Latrobe, and Bruce Doolan. Our players were getting very excited. I was sitting at the far end of the huge Melbourne dressing room and I could see the tension and nerves in the next batsmen due to go in, Trevor Docking, Peter Roberts, Stephen Howard. Maybe nerves overcame them for Jim Higgs, a leg spinner, picked up three middle-order wickets and we were starting to wobble. I could see the tension creeping up so I casually went downstairs and put my pads on and moved myself up the order from eight to six. All I had in my mind was to stay there; we needed to play just a normal game and keep wickets in hand for the last ten overs and there shouldn't be a problem. I saw Walker through to the end of his overs but our middle order of four wickets contributed 14 runs between them and we were threatening to collapse. I thought we can't get so close and lose. Mansfield, God bless him, was the one who stayed with me and we got to the last two overs — eight-ball overs — with 16 needed, a run a ball. We only had two batsmen to come, one who wasn't regarded too much as a batsman (Les Appleton) but could play fairly straight and block and Gary Whitney, who was more nervous than the other ten put together. I didn't expect us to have too much chance if Whitney had to come in, at least if he was on strike. We did well in Thomson's last over, hitting him for ten to bring us within six runs of the first-ever win for Tasmania in the five years we had been in the Gillette Cup. I was on strike for that last over, thinking eight balls to come, six to win, we shouldn't have any problems at all. Naturally I was used to heart-stoppers with Lancashire — if you can ever be said to get used to them — and I suppose I was calm in comparison to the scenes apparently going on in the dressing room. I didn't score off the first ball and got a single off the second. Mansfield hit the third ball to long on, I called two and if Sieler, who was bowling the final over, had taken the return cleanly at the stumps, I would have been run out. But it was a chance worth taking and now we needed three off five balls with Mansfield on strike again. He went down the wicket to the fourth ball and was stumped and I was disappointed he had left his crease that way at such a stage. Now we needed three runs from four balls and I met Appleton as he walked out and said as casually as I could: "Looks like we have a good chance of winning this, Les." He was always very tanned with a light brown skin but at this moment he was as white as a paper sheet. He said: "I'm just going to get one Jack. You can have the strike and I'm not coming down to that end again." I couldn't believe him. I said: "No, hang on a minute, Les. If Redpath brings the field in to attempt to stop me getting the strike, you have to go at hitting through the field or over the top because we need a four and we've won." And he said again:

"Jack, I'm just getting one." He took guard, 6ft. 3in. of him, and all he did was put his foot down the wicket, blocked the ball and ran like hell. Naturally, I was backing up quite a lot and I was much faster in those days so I got in comfortably.

Now Tasmania had three balls to get two runs to win their first Gillette tie with Simmons on strike and Appleton at the other end. Then Redpath, who had seldom altered his field to meet the changing requirements of the innings, surprised me again. I felt certain he would bring somebody close to stop us blocking and running again. But he didn't. He was fielding at extra cover thirty yards away so I hit the next ball at him and ran down the track shouting to Les: "One!" which would have left him two balls to get a single. But he just put his hand up and said "No". And he wouldn't run. So I went down the wicket and said to him: "Now that's a bit stupid, Les." He said: "Jack, if I go down that end, there's no way I'll be able to grip the bat to hit the ball. I'm so nervous all I want to do is run. I'll run as fast as I possibly can and I'll run for a two. But I'm not running anything else." And he meant it. The seventh ball was angled across me outside off stump and the only place I thought I could hit it was either wide of extra cover or over him but even then I thought Higgs at long off might be round quickly. I attempted to hit it over the top and missed it. Everybody was now so keyed up. We needed two off the last ball and even then Redpath hardly altered his field. If he had dropped the fielders back ten to fifteen yards there was no way we would have been able to run two, and I would have had to hit it a lot further in the air to get it over the top. Redpath kept the same field, Sieler tried the same ball and I went for the same shot and luckily for me I hit it quite high over extra cover and Higgs, with no chance of catching it, ran round but only got a finger tip to it as it went one bounce for four. We'd won. I could hardly believe it. As I had taken guard for the last ball I had said: "Please God, don't let us get to this position and not win." If we had got a single we would have lost by having more wickets down. I walked off crying with all their lads coming up and shaking hands and when I looked up to the dressing room from the middle of the M.C.G. all I could see was a stream of players and committee men running down the gangway onto the Oval. It was a very moving scene. I thought I was a bit unlucky not to get the Man of the Match after taking one for 31 and scoring 37 not out at a time when it was really needed. But it was given to a bowler, Kevin Badcock, who had bowled really well for one for 14 in his eight overs. It didn't worry me then but afterwards I thought I would have got it in England. The match was televised in Tasmania but was not recorded so it wasn't kept and has not been seen again. It sparked off a great deal of interest in Tasmanian cricket, people were stopping me in the streets and when I went to the schools I definitely had to go in and have a cup of tea before and after coaching. That, I found, was the biggest difference for me but what it meant to the rest of the lads cannot be measured. It made them realise they had the ability to win, they knew how to win, and this was the first step to getting into the Sheffield Shield competition.

Victory took us into the semi-final where we played New Zealand and lost. But they had a Test side, not just a state side, and they had always taken part to help make up the numbers. We were put into bat and scored 176 of which Stephen Howard hit 51. To me he was a miniature Doug Walters but didn't have enough confidence in his own ability. That was Tasmania's biggest problem. I knew if their players had been playing for Lancashire with a lot of professionals round them they'd soon have got into the groove and become far better players. I didn't think we'd done that badly and though we lost by seven wickets we made them struggle for a while. A disappointing factor about the match was that the game was played at Melbourne and only 2,900 watched. If that had been played at Launceston, Hobart or Devonport there'd have been 10,000 or 12,000 people watching. I thought the Board and the sponsors were crackers to take the game to Melbourne. We were always regarded as down and outs in Australian cricket and what gave me as much pleasure as anything was that after we'd beaten Victoria, despite losing to New Zealand, we weren't regarded as a joke from then on. People said we were going to improve and the more first-class cricket we could get the better for everybody concerned with Australian cricket. A point I had been making over and over had been proved; we had the ability and while we might not have had the depth of talent of other states we still had capable players who would have made it more quickly and probably been more successful if they had been with other states. Howard impressed me as a very talented player but one who was overawed just by the thought of playing against first-class cricketers. But the more you played, the better you became. When he and Bruce Doolan had bad spells, the selectors immediately decided Tasmania wouldn't progress with older players and must go for younger ones. I thought this was a bad step and maybe that sort of policy had occurred not just at Tasmania but at Lancashire, too, and we both seemed to have made the same mistakes.

During that season the touring side was England and although it was my home country coming with players I knew, by now I had such an affinity to Tasmanian cricket that if I could pull the wool over some of the English players' eyes I would enjoy it, especially with two Lancastrians, David Lloyd and Peter Lever, there. But England weren't having that good a time in the Test series against Lillee and Thomson and Co. The wicket at Launceston hadn't been playing too well and was on the green side and trying to outdo Mike Denness, England's captain, I said: "Mike, it doesn't matter to me whether we bat or bowl. If you want to win the toss I'll arrange it." I hoped England would bat but Denness said no, he felt his bowlers needed a run. So he put us in which was what I didn't want to happen. Even so I thought our lads were a bit more used to the conditions and could take better advantage. Peter Lever, Geoff Arnold and Chris Old bowled and after about an hour Lever left the field and came to the dressing room. "Jack, this wicket's a little bit too bad," he said. "You have a very important game coming up against New Zealand (our semi-final) and we feel if we come in off our long runs we could hurt some of your players." Maybe Peter had been sent by Denness, maybe they thought if they went off a fifteen yard run-up I would do the same which would give them an advantage with their years of John Player League cricket where run-ups are restricted to that length. But I felt obliged. They bowled us out for 164 and I was caught at second slip off Arnold who was as hard to handle off fifteen yards as he would have been off his normal run. We were trying out bowlers and in the opening overs the ball seamed and bounced. David Lloyd got one or two round his ears and didn't enjoy it. He played a few shots and was caught on the fine leg boundary. Keith Fletcher didn't last too long and I had to admit it was a bad wicket and I was feeling for England who were going towards the fifth Test at Adelaide. I also felt for our bowlers who were trying to get the remaining spot in the Tasmanian state side, so rather than ask them to slow down, I took them off. I put on Kevin Badcock, a medium pacer, and myself when Denness and Brian Luckhurst were batting and though both batsmen were hit a few times in the ribs and on the hands they got runs. I thought they'd declare about 250, around 80 ahead and then try to bowl us out, but they just batted on and on and by the time I realised what was happening the ball was soft, life had gone from the wicket, and although I brought the quickies back the batsmen handled everything confidently and went on to reach 341 for four declared with Denness getting a century.

A few comments were made to me that I had helped keep Denness in his job as England captain for longer than some thought he should have been. What really disgusted me was that I felt they'd taken advantage of my decision to take the quickies off. If I'd left them on we would have run through the England side. And when we went in again, expecting them to bowl off their John Player run as in the first innings, they went to their long runs and bowled us out to win by an innings and 72 runs. I thought: What a fool you've been, Simmo, you've been conned, not just in allowing Denness to get runs and get back into the England side after dropping himself at Sydney, but in being heavily defeated. Being conned really annoyed me. They weren't worried once they had enough runs. They didn't want to bat again and didn't worry whether they hit us and hurt us in the second innings. They all bowled off long runs and I thought that was the last time I would ever be influenced by my place of birth. I knew I had been attempting to con Denness in the first place, but not to the extent that I thought we could win. It might have helped us to have bowled first on that wicket, to at least have made it a real game over three days, and everybody would have been pleased with Tasmania's performance instead of being stuffed by Mike Denness. So I always vowed to myself after that, even if my good friend, Clive Lloyd, was involved, and he had said he would like batting practice for his players, I'd have said: "If you win the toss Clive, you have the choice." And when I thought of Tasmanian cricket I knew that was what I was employed to do, and that was what I was going to do. So I learned something from that and probably earned respect from the Tasmanian players. We were getting more professional in our outlook.

In 1976 I got David Hughes, my good mate at Lancashire, the post of Tasmania Cricket Council coach in Hobart, a similar job to mine. They treated players as employees down there, just like Lancashire did many years ago — "You work for us, son, you'll do as we say." David said he would coach the entire area but told Jules Murfett, a state selector, that they would have to provide the balls. Jules produced two boxes of used balls, some good, some not so good, and said: "I don't want any of these lost and I want them back in the same condition." David was going for six weeks and was coaching about fifty youngsters every day! There was not enough consideration of people by the T.C.C. who got their priorities wrong too often, and fell down on little things that made such a bad impression but which could have been so easily rectified. During a Tasmania game at Hobart, David, who wasn't playing in the game, wasn't invited to lunch. And he was the T.C.C. coach. The same thing happened to Graeme Fowler when he went there. I was commentator at the game and having lunch with two colleagues when Graeme came in and was asked to sit with us. He asked the chairman if he could have lunch and it was refused. It was so petty. I just left my lunch and went to one of the stalls and had a pie with Graeme.

David Hughes played a time or two for Tasmania and in one game in Brisbane against Queensland in a Gillette Cup match, the two of us were batting together when Jeff Thomson was bowling. He was really letting it fly, getting bounce and making the ball rear at David's chin. In the course of a maiden over, David must have played and missed four times in eight balls and at the end of the over we had a chat, deciding Thomson would probably bowl only one more over, maybe two, and save two for the end. "Can't you get a one and come down this end?" David asked me. I said I wasn't really worried about leaving my end, it wasn't quite so hard facing Greg Chappell. David was still down the other end when Thomson started his next over and the first ball flew past his nose. He managed to play one down to third man and as we crossed he said: "Thank God for that. At least you can have a go now." Thomson dug the next ball in shorter and as I leaned back to let it go, the ball ran down the face of the bat to third man for a single. David groaned as we ran: "I can't believe this." Thomson was giving us some abuse. "You bloody Poms can't bat," he said. I was at the non-striker's end but I wasn't going to tell a bowler who delivers at about ninety miles an hour where to get off. "I couldn't agree with you more, Thommo," I said. "We're not batting well at all, are we?" He didn't say much after that!

10
INTO THE SHEFFIELD SHIELD

It was during my sixth season in Tasmania, in 1977–78, that the island was allowed into Australia's Sheffield Shield competition, although it was only on a trial basis with one game against each of the other states, giving us five matches in the season to everybody else's nine. Still, we were delighted. Half a chance is better than none at all and we had certainly been improving through the years I had been there. Not that I'm saying I had anything to do with it! When I returned to England in March, 1977, I heard that Yorkshire's John Hampshire, who had had two years in Hobart before I ever went out, was to be signed as their overseas player. I was highly delighted because I had always got on well with him, and he had a good sense of humour. I liked his attitude to the game and his Yorkshire competitiveness was something we were going to need. During our first Roses match in May he hinted that he was almost certain to be Tasmanian captain, not that that worried me too much. I just wanted to be a member of that side out of pride. I had played with Tasmania for five years, had never before played four-day cricket and I was looking forward to the challenge. Nothing had been said to me, either by letter or phone, but I thought, well, if that's the case, I couldn't be under a better captain than John Hampshire. Anyway, when I got back out there in October 1977, more trial games had been arranged and everybody was looking forward to making history.

The side for the opening game was announced after the trials and it was one of my proudest moments in cricket to be named captain of Tasmania's first Sheffield Shield team. I don't know whether Hampshire was disappointed but he was the first to congratulate me. He was made vice-captain and I couldn't have wished for anything better. Our first game was as tough as could be, but everybody was still pleased we were going to Perth to take on Western Australia because they had been the last state before us to get into the Sheffield Shield, many years earlier. So we were welcomed probably more warmly by the W.A. committee and players than if we had gone to any other state, knowing what we were going to have to go through if we were to qualify as full-time members. But at that time they were the best, most professional side in Australia. The Tasmania Cricket Council had done their homework and signed a medium fast bowler called Dennis Baker who came from Western Australia and had played in about fifteen Shield games. With Baker helping the likes of Garry Cowmeadow and Rowan Sherriff and possibly Gary Whitney, this was going to be a better balanced side than before, except perhaps in the spinning department. We knew how hard it was going to be and the T.C.C. decided to do it properly and take us over four days early to get acclimatised and help us become accustomed to those fast, bouncy Perth wickets.

The welcome we got from the Western Australia Cricket Association and the Mayor of Perth was tremendous, the sort of reception Tasmanian players had not experienced before. The only thing against us was that it rained for three of the four days. This was not a game for youngsters and the team chosen was quite strong and experienced — Jack Simmons, John Hampshire, Dennis Baker, Tony Benneworth, Garry Cowmeadow, Trevor Docking, Bruce Doolan, Stephen Howard, Bruce Neill, Mickey Norman, and Rowan Sherriff and David Smith. Neill was possibly lucky to be chosen — he had put in some class performances in club games but had got a "duck" in a trial; Norman was a determined young man who had gone to England to try to improve; and Sherriff I thought, was a very good left-arm swing bowler but didn't have the strength to come back over four days so after Baker and Cowmeadow, I knew I was going to have to play a big part, even when the wicket didn't suit me. I found that in the early games bad line and length were smashed by Shield players, then Joe

Soap had to come up and put the brake on as much as I could.

We lost the toss and with all the rain there had been it was no surprise when John Inverarity, the W.A. captain, put us in to bat. Leg spinner Tony Mann, a player I had seen many times in England when he was professional with Bacup in the Lancashire League, took five for 43 and we were bowled out for 147. There was a tremendous thunderstorm on the second morning that left half the ground under water but the umpires decided to have an early lunch with a view to starting soon after. The flood had subsided, of course, but even so the ground was still saturated and I couldn't believe the umpires' decision. I knew we were the Cinderella state but there was no way I was going to be steam-rollered into playing. I rolled a ball next to the wicket and spray shot up twelve inches. I asked the umpires if they really believed it was fit to start and they said they had to try to get the game underway, and that the wicket itself wasn't wet. I agreed the pitch wasn't wet but it only needed a few defensive shots and the ball would be like a wet rag and that wouldn't be fair to us, the fielding side. Luckily, Inverarity agreed with me, so the umpires relented. Whether they were trying to put one over on Tasmania, the nonentities, I don't know. As Tasmania had played only one first-class game a season before that, I hadn't come across too many Australian umpires, but I'd heard quite a lot from Peter Lever, David Lloyd and the England side when they'd been out and from Clive Lloyd, and what I'd heard had led me to believe they weren't the best umpires in the world. I didn't think Tasmanian umpires were either, so I wasn't being biased or parochial. I was grateful to Inverarity, a fine cricketer, an honest man and one of the best ambassadors Australian cricket ever had, for persuading the umpires not to even think of looking at the ground until after lunch. Soon after we started in the afternoon, Graeme Wood, the W.A. opener, hooked a bouncer from Cowmeadow and Howard, one of our best fielders, only had ten or fifteen yards to run for a steepling catch, yet slipped on his back and didn't get a touch on the ball. I couldn't resist saying to the umpire as we passed: "Yes, it is fair to both sides, isn't it?" He called me back and said we couldn't continue to call the game off just because it was a little bit wet in one area. I said I thought they should have taken into consideration that it was our first game in the Shield and that they could have asked the curator to dry certain spots. In the end we lost by an innings after Terry Alderman had taken four for 32 in our second innings, a disheartening start on the surface of things, but I knew everybody was nervy and finding it difficult to settle down. I had been playing a long time for Lancashire then and I felt the pressure so I knew the tensions the amateur cricketers of Tasmania were feeling. Even Hampshire mentioned to me he felt nervous, especially against Western Australia in Perth. Because we were playing only five games to the other states' nine, our bonus points from the match were multiplied by nine and divided by five, taking our three points — Western Australia got 21 — to 5.4!

Even more than the game itself I remember that trip for another reason. That was the first year of Kerry Packer and World Series cricket and Dennis Lillee, one of the very many who had joined and who were banned from playing Shield games, had practised on a school ground next door to the W.A.C.A. ground in Perth. Lillee asked me if there were two or three Tasmanian batsmen who would like to bat against him and other Packer players. It was all unofficial and we did it early in the evening on the quiet for we might well have been kicked out of the Sheffield Shield before we'd bowled a ball if anybody had got to know about it. I felt it was a good opportunity for some of our youngsters, particularly David Smith, our twelfth man, to face the great man. I went across to the school and bowled to Ross Edwards and Bruce Laird and they were all grateful to us for giving them our time. We were hoping to go across again the following night but the Tasmanian manager-cum-selector, Alan Carey, asked me about it and said it would not be looked on too kindly by the Board. I pointed out that it was good practice for our players, but phone calls must have been exchanged with Tasmania and the following morning a directive was issued by Carey who said the T.C.C. had ordered that no player was to practise with the World Series players. So I had to tell Lillee we were sorry but we couldn't jeopardise our lads' chances of playing in Shield cricket.

Our second Shield game was in Melbourne against Victoria and we lost that one as well, not by an innings but by nine wickets. At least we were improving! Victoria scored 377 of which Paul Melville, who looked a very good player, scored 70. He had played as professional with Rishton in the Lancashire League at home, a popular lad who looked to have a fine future in the game. Unfortunately he developed a brain tumour and died the following year at a very early age.

It was around this time that I discovered that Dennis Baker was being paid 15,000 dollars by the T.C.C. for the five Shield games. I had never been paid to play for Tasmania through the years and all I had received, like everybody else, had been out-of-pocket expenses and meal allowance which I think, when we went into the Shield, was twenty-five dollars a day. Hampshire was employed to play for Tasmania and when he didn't, he coached. I was slightly different, being employed to coach and perhaps play, if selected. During the Victorian innings I bowled about 40 overs in a temperature over 100 degrees and I had to lie down afterwards, I was so tired. Hampshire said he thought I was crackers to play without being paid when Baker was getting all that money just for five games. "I haven't too much of a grievance," he said. "They asked me how much I wanted and near enough gave it to me. But I think it is diabolical that you, as captain, shouldn't be paid as an overseas player along with me." So we went to see the chairman, Max Gillett, a very nice, amiable person, maybe too parochial for the position he held because he came from the south and saw many things in a biased way. The secretary, Peter Hadlow, was there as well and Hampshire, who was receiving about half Baker's fee, which shows how ludicrous it all was, did most of the talking. Gillett repeated what Hampshire had said about him having no comeback for he had stated his own terms and they had been met. As far as I was concerned, they said, the N.T.C.A. were my employers and the T.C.C. had no jurisdiction over the matter. I felt more hurt than annoyed, the feeling that I was being used by the T.C.C. while somebody else, nowhere near as experienced, was being paid colossal money. I know it perhaps had to compensate for him going over to the island and having to get a house, but I was a professional cricketer and felt I was being used. I wasn't asking anything near Baker's figure and if they had said they would pay me just 1,000 dollars for the five games, I'd have been tickled pink. But they seemed to take the view that I'd been there a long time, was part of the furniture, and I had been given the captaincy, so I didn't get any further with the chairman though I felt I might have done if I'd been coach in the south instead of the north. I don't think I've ever allowed anything off the field to upset my concentration on it and after bowling all those overs and taken two for 59, I took the only second innings wicket to fall by getting Julien Wiener out.

We had lost our first two Shield games but we were feeling more confident, especially as the other three were to be played in Tasmania. But the real change in our attitude and approach, not just in the players, but in committee and spectators and people in Tasmania, came in the two matches we played against the touring Indian team. They had a marvellous series that season against Australia who were being captained by Bobby Simpson, making a comeback after the defection of so many Australian players to Kerry Packer. They were beaten by Western Australia but had taken other states apart and were specially strong in spinners with Bishen Bedi, Chandrasekhar, Prasanna and Venkat. India came to Tasmania to help us raise money and played a one-day game in Launceston and a four-day match in Hobart. Sunil Gavaskar captained the side in Bedi's absence and arranged his batting order for the one-day game to allow his players practice and put himself in the middle of the order. Their early batsmen did not do too well, including Surinder Amarnath who was hit in the mouth by a ball from Cowmeadow and had to have teeth extracted. It needed a partnership from Mohinder Amarnath and Gavaskar, who punished me quite heavily, to get India to 170. All our players got into double figures except for one of the openers, and it was left to Benneworth to hit the winning runs with five balls to spare, a six over mid wicket. It was a great thrill and showed what the lads could do because we had needed 48 runs off the last six eight-ball overs.

I think Gavaskar had gone into the game with too much

confidence, expecting to win easily, and most of their Test players were included when we played the four-day match at Hobart. I declared at 267 for eight just before stumps on the first day and the following day we went to town on them, bowling them out for 189 with their last five wickets falling for 19 runs. Baker bowled well but I came up trumps, too, as I finished with four for 11 off seven overs. I felt I had to go on because Madan Lal was starting to get runs and I wanted to quieten it down at one end and let the pace bowlers go with the wind at the other. I had Madan Lal caught and bowled about ankle height and although I said the catch had carried to me, he wasn't sure and waited for the umpire who said he couldn't see because I was in the way. I've never cheated anybody in my life and I wasn't going to start then, in an international match, but fortunately the square leg umpire had seen it and gave him out. So we got a good first innings lead of 78 but in the last hour and a half Ghavri brought us to our knees with some fine pace bowling which left us 55 for four overnight with Blair Campbell and me as night watchmen. We were bowled out for 101 on the third day, Ghavri taking seven for 49, which emphasised one of Tasmania's faults, the relaxing in concentration over a four-day match. I thought we were throwing the game away with bad batting after we'd got a good first innings lead. What pleased me was that their seam bowlers had done the damage with movement off the wicket which fortunately continued for us. They only needed 180 to win but we bowled them out for 95 with Baker running through them for five for 45. Another highlight for me was a catch by Docking to dismiss Ashok Mankad, an astonishing gulley catch, which must be the best I've ever seen.

It was a wonderful win and the excitement was tremendous with people coming up to me and handing over ten and twenty dollars for the lads to have a drink. I know the wickets weren't all they should have been, the Hobart one having uneven bounce and seaming all the time. Rain kept the wicket juicy with a little dampness through the three days and while the wicket might have been blamed who was bothered? We had proved that bit better in the conditions and that was one of the best days of my career. To be captain of the side that beat India — twice — I just had to be a very happy man. As the game had ended on the third of the four days the T.C.C. allowed us to stay and celebrate and go home the following day. We went to a pub not far from the ground where the landlord, I understood, was from Yorkshire. He left twenty dollars as well so we all had a drink there with Hampshire and me, being Poms, being given pint glasses. The Australian beer is far stronger than English and I don't think drinking out of pint glasses was really all that good an idea. It wasn't long before I was feeling the effects and I wasn't allowed to drive when we finished off the night at the Wrest Point casino with yours truly falling asleep in the reception area.

Our next match was in the Gillette Cup against South Australia, also at Hobart, and after those wins over India we were brimming over with confidence like Tasmania had never seen before. We were put in to bat by South Australian captain Bob Blewett, an accomplished all-rounder. We were struggling badly at one stage at 117 for six and I went in and hit 36 in 31 minutes to help us reach 184, not a big total but a realistic one. One-day cricket seems to bring the best out of me. I enjoy it so much and maybe it is more my type of play as a batsman who likes to hit the ball and a bowler who can keep it tight. I hit ten off one over from Stillman and 14 off Attenborough including a big six over mid-wicket as we added 48 off the last five overs. They made a terrible start and slipped to 25 for five after Baker had dismissed the first two batsmen for "ducks". Rick Darling was playing well and he had a chance of getting into the Test team which seemed to be more on his mind than the result of our match. There was no way he could take risks in that situation, of course, and South Australia had recovered to 133 for six in 33 overs when a gale force wind came up and rain drove us off. The scores and wickets were identical at the corresponding stage in each innings and we tried to work out who would win if the game ended there. But we were able to go back out and they had seven overs in which to score 52, but they just didn't seem bothered. They let the scoring rate sag so that they wanted well over a run a ball at one time. I positioned everybody on the boundary edge except the wicketkeeper, everybody in a position to save two runs, and we just kept putting South Australia further and further behind the scoring rate so that all they managed in the end was 167. Darling was probably happy with it all for he reached his 100 in the last over and did get into the Test side. Blewett, who was not the best of losers, didn't bother with the after-match presentations until it came to the stage of handing over 500 dollars to the losing side. Then he came out of the dressing room, took the cheque and went back in again, without waiting to see who was named Man of the Match — Darling. Blewett complained about the conditions, about the wind and the rain and said we should have waited longer before going back on the field. Then when I talked to him in the bar after the game he was as nice as ninepence — a funny guy. So that gave us three wins in a row and I couldn't have been happier. I had bowled well, too, taking one for 12 in my eight overs, four of which were maidens, one of my best performances. The South Australian manager, Geoff Noblet, who had played with Nelson in the Lancashire League, came to me and apologised for the behaviour of Blewett. He said we were the better side on the day.

Our next match in the Gillette Cup was at Melbourne where we had secured our first win three years earlier over Victoria. There was a lot of pre-match publicity and Peter McFarlane, writing in the *Melbourne Age*, said Victoria had the big guns for the game but if anybody could repeat the win of 1974, he said, it was Jack Simmons. And I did so want us to win just to show that the 1974 result was no flash in the pan, that we were now a side to be reckoned with. After three successive victories our batsmen were beginning to believe in themselves and we started well against Ian Callan and Alan Hurst after being put in to bat. Hampshire didn't like opening the innings but said if I thought it was best for the side he would do it and he and Bruce Doolan, put on 50 for the first wicket. Howard batted well for 61, Docking hit a quick 30 and we came up with a good total of 224, five and a half runs an over which certainly wasn't beyond Victoria's experienced side which had three Test players, Paul Hibbert, Julien Wiener, and Graham Yallop in their early order. In fact it was a team bursting with players who had either played Test cricket or were soon going to and I knew it was going to be hard. Wiener scored 71 and looked to be the one who was going to win it for them until I came up with one of the best spells of bowling I've had. They had been keeping up with the five and a half runs an over rate so I came on to try to frustrate Dav Whatmore and keep everything tighter. Straightaway he drove a catch to Hampshire at mid-wicket. Now for Yallop who could take the game right away from us if he stayed any length of time. I hadn't dropped mid-on back and I tied Yallop down until he decided to go for the big hit over mid-on, a place where he liked to hit me. Cowmeadow was fielding there, a footballer as well, fit as a fiddle and looking like Mister Universe, and he turned and ran ten to fifteen yards before diving full length to hold on to the catch. I always had help from the fielders and that was a marvellous catch. It was a very hot day and Wiener was sweating like a pig as he ran some fine, quick singles. But once he was out and Melville was run out, the Vics fell apart and lost their last seven wickets for 59 runs to lose by 37 runs. We had bowled them out for 187 and won with four overs to spare and I thought we should have had the Man of the Match, too, in Howard. It would have done him the world of good and raised his confidence even more. But it was given to Wiener.

We were a happy band in the dressing room and as it was Sunday with no pubs open in Melbourne in those days, we just stayed and drank the fridge dry before going back to the hotel. Yallop said some kind, generous things after the match, saying anything could happen in one-day cricket and with the spirit we'd got after four successive wins, who would dare say that Tasmania couldn't beat Western Australia in the final, even in Perth where playing there was like an extra man to the W.A. side. I was pleased, too, that the newspapers the following morning said we had won convincingly and deservingly, no mention of a one-off, a flash in the pan. The publicity we were now getting was fantastic with headings about like "Jack's Giant-Killers". Lou Richards wrote in Melbourne that cricket's smarties said it was a bit of a joke when Tasmania were admitted to Sheffield Shield cricket and that the Apple Isle had finally got in under sufferance and it was only a sympathy vote. "But the Taswegians have bowled the critics with the best yorker since their own Max Walker played real Test cricket," he wrote. "And they tell me the curator still hasn't mowed the turf where Tasmania beat India last month. What's more, Tassie captain Jack Simmons is already crowing his boys will knock off South Australia in the coming Sheffield Shield match as well as take the Gillette Cup. I think Simmo could be talking through his glass of apple cider to make a prediction like that." If you can't crow after four wins in a row, albeit three of them in one-day games, you can't crow about anything, and I couldn't say I wasn't confident of beating South Australia, could I? What good would that have done the rest of the side? But Lou did say he wouldn't argue with an old pro like me . . . "a true pro at 36, so he should know where to start to build a first-class team." Good old Lou, I could have done with him on my shoulder all the time.

During the period between the semi-final and the final I was invited to a dinner by the chairman of the Australian Cricket Board in honour of the 1977–78 Indian touring side. It was held in Adelaide on 26 January 1978 and I was thrilled to bits because not only the Test players were there, but Sir Don Bradman as well. On my way home, while I was waiting at Adelaide airport, there was a tannoy message asking me to go to reception for a phone call. It was the Press. "What did I think about the appeal and Mrs Luck?" I hadn't heard about any appeal or Mrs Luck and it turned out that while I was away, the N.T.C.A., through Tom Room, had announced on television that they had spent 200,000 dollars on ground improvements and were getting desperate for sponsorship to bring me back for my seventh year. Unless there was help, it would probably be my last year. Within twenty-four hours this very nice and fine old lady who had given a lot of money to other sporting organisations, came up with 5,000 dollars. Mrs Dell Luck had given tens of thousands of dollars to charities in Devonport where she lived, mainly to handicapped children, but also to sport, to surfing and that funny sport where men walk up and down the beach wearing trunks and a tight cap, the Devonport Surf Life-Saving

Club. After Tom Room's TV appearance one of the first calls to the N.T.C.A. office and to Cedric Knight, the secretary, was from Mrs Luck with her 5,000 dollars. One condition was that she would like to meet me because she wanted to tell me she thought I was doing such a lot for Tasmania and for young people.

When I returned I learned she was in hospital, so I took some flowers to her and she was so pleased. Both she and her husband became quite good friends of ours and we used to go to their house. She died in my last year, 1983–84, and I was invited to the funeral of a beautiful and very generous lady. When I met her in hospital I asked why she had given 5,000 dollars and she said she knew somebody would want to beat it. She thought it was great for kids to be coached and kept off streets, doing something that would do them good. Mrs Luck was proved right for a day or two after her donation the Launceston Bank for Savings came in with 10,000 dollars over two years. It all made you feel very humble, especially all the small donations that came in, like one old man who went to the chairman and said it was important Tasmania kept Jack Simmons and how could he help. He was told the only thing people could do was make donations so he told the chairman he was a pensioner, "But here," he said. "Here's ten dollars." And apparently that was typical of a lot of people. Naturally, the big ones got all the publicity like dear Mrs Luck, a beaut old lady, very smart, and when asked by the Press about her offering, said: "There's no pockets in caskets. And it's no good taking it with you. I'd sooner see the good that can be done with donations than leave it to somebody in my will." When I met her I realised how sincere she was. She said when she saw the win over Victoria it hit her that maybe Tasmania wouldn't be as good a side and be able to do so well if Jack Simmons wasn't playing.

The N.T.C.A. said they had to raise 8,500 dollars or they lose Jack Simmons. Perhaps a lot of people thought that was my salary but it wasn't. It also incorporated air tickets and our flat which took about half the money, leaving my salary of about 4,000 dollars and a few expenses which I needed as I was being taxed twice — in Australia and England. Naturally I had to do things for the Launceston Bank for Savings in return for their 10,000 dollars: there were lifesize cut-outs of me being Father Christmas to appeal to youngsters to open savings accounts — I enjoyed that, it was something different; a photo taken with the general manager, Mr Bugg; my accounts were transferred from other banks to theirs and it turned out to be an enjoyable sponsorship and association as they helped with the reconstruction of the coaching system, they paid for cricket bags, different-size cricket bats, pads and gloves, which must have cost them at least another thousand. The chairman of the bank, Ray Farrell, who was knighted the following year, had been a good cricketer in his time and he became a good friend and we played a few matches together.

Other business houses in the town gave money: the Enfield Hotel 200 dollars, which was marvellous; Mrs Waterhouse gave 50, Mr Peters 30, Mr Bennett 10, the Crown Hotel Sports Club 100, Mr Thors 50, Mr Hills 10 and just before we went to the final at Perth another appeal went out and an 83-year-old pensioner who was listed as anonymous, gave 25 dollars. It doesn't half make you feel good when that sort of thing happens and I know I had been overwhelmed ever since hearing about it at Adelaide airport when I choked up on hearing about Mrs Luck. When I told Jacqueline what it was about she started crying and there were the two of us, the Simmonses, bawling in Adelaide airport. It showed that a lot of people felt something for you and appreciated what you were trying to do. Graham Mansfield, a former Tasmanian teammate and who was coach on the north-west coast, wrote that Simmons was worth 15,000 dollars and said if they spent that to get me back the following summer, it would be money well spent. But he assured everybody that the cost of getting me back wouldn't be anything near that. A lot of interest had been stirred up through our successes and the appeal and because we were the Cinderellas of the Gillette Cup final John Hampshire and I were asked to go to Perth two days earlier than the rest of the side just to do promotion work for Gillette. We didn't get a fee but we were looked after and they were pleased with the help we gave them.

We were under a great disadvantage in having to go to Perth to play the final, especially against a Western Australian side that had hardly any weaknesses in it. John Inverarity, one of the very nicest people I've ever had the good fortune to meet, and Ian Brayshaw, who I had known from his days in the Lancashire League with Bacup, were involved in the promotion with us, two players who had given W.A. wonderful service through the years. We started early, 9.30 or 10 a.m., much too early for me. I've never enjoyed getting up first thing in the morning. We thought a Perth wicket with its bounce and pace was going to be a disadvantage to us but it wasn't as quick as we anticipated, perhaps because of the weather they had had, but it was still quicker than any others we'd played on. According to all reports there were 14,000 people there including a lot of Tasmanians or exiled Tasmanians with banners, plus television and radio.

Inverarity put us in and we batted reasonably well for our 184 for nine off 40 eight-ball overs with Roger Woolley, in only his second match, scoring 56. We had talked about not pulling or hooking the ball because the pace might be more than we were used to and our openers, Hampshire and Doolan, who both liked to have a go, restrained themselves until they had seen off the new ball and were feeling good. Then, to our dismay, they both played the hook shot to balls that rose more steeply than they expected and one was caught by the wicket-keeper, the other in the slips. Woolley played well, confident and courageous and showing his great potential, and at the end of the 35th over we were 151 with a chance of reaching 200. Inverarity bowled himself in the last over, left-arm spin that brought him three wickets and kept our total down. Inverarity had done a thoroughly good job as captain in field placings and bowling changes and the W.A. fielding was excellent. In our post mortem on the way home we reckoned they saved between 20 and 30 runs with their athleticism and keenness and I learned again the value of fielding, of diving and saving runs on the boundary edge, turning fours into twos and threes. So the Tasmanian lads learned a lot from the W.A. fielding and this helped us the following year when we got through to the final again. It also showed the value of sitting and talking over a game, that there is always something for everybody to learn. We bowled badly at the start and W.A. had reached 50 off nine overs and as usual when that happened I went on and tried to cut it back a bit. Benneworth was a similar type, line and length, and we did manage to stop them running away with the game. In our pre-match talks Baker, who had played with W.A., said Ric Charlesworth and Graeme Wood took chances when they were running, that they would hit straight to a fielder and still run. I couldn't believe this was exactly true but they were such a good pair, good runners, that they took the risks and it worked out for them. We did run Charlesworth out for 33, but by then W.A. had reached 107! I got Kim Hughes out for a "duck" but there was no stopping Wood who went on to his century as W.A. won quite comfortably with three overs to spare. We weren't disgraced and Inverarity was good to us in his interviews with the Press and on television and radio. We were disappointed but happy we had put up a courageous effort that was very creditable. During that time, one of the nicest things that happened to us was that the Tasmanian premier, Mr Doug Law, a quiet, unassuming, honest man who was keen on cricket, either attended games or sent us telegrams. One congratulated us on the team's great effort in beating Victoria and another, five days later, promised us a state reception when we won our first Sheffield Shield match. Unfortunately, it didn't come that year although we did manage to draw our three games in Tasmania after losing to Western Australia and Victoria.

I felt Tasmania had had a good season in 1977–78, their first in the Sheffield Shield. All the players except David Smith and Roger Woolley had been around for some time, but it fell to new boy Woolley, to score the first Shield 100 for Tasmania, against Queensland at Launceston when we scored 329 for five declared. Woolley loved the publicity that came with it and the following day, when everybody was going out for practice before the start of the third day's play, he was still in his tracksuit, having photos taken, lounging about, and not bothering with nets. Early wickets fell in the second innings and Woolley joined Hampshire about half an hour before lunch and was out for a "duck". When he came in, Hampshire said he hoped I wouldn't mind him saying a few words, but he felt they had to be said. Four days was hard for Tasmanian youngsters to concentrate and put everything into the game and we believed if we didn't tell them of their faults and instruct them there was no way they were going to learn. Hampshire said Woolley had been strutting about in his tracksuit thinking he knew it all after his 103, and told him he still had plenty to learn. He laced into others as well for not concentrating hard enough and put over the point that one innings doesn't make a batsman. To get 100, a magnificent achievement though it might be, especially the first one, it just showed you couldn't relax, for the next time you went in you would only be as good as that score. In Woolley's case it was a "duck" probably because of over-confidence and lack of thought for the side. I've seen it happen with quite a lot of youngsters, get to their 100, and think they've done their job. It was ten minutes before any of the players were allowed out of the dressing room and Hampshire put his point over in a typically blunt Northern way — a good rollicking for everybody to hear, for everybody to learn from. He even told me off because I hadn't been out to practise at the same time. "I know you have a lot of other things to do as captain," he said, "but sometimes it can be more beneficial to the side to be with them." There were things I had to do on behalf of the N.T.C.A. but he was right, the players were my concern. We did assess the team and look at problems because there was a huge difference in approach now we were in the Sheffield Shield.

When we lost to Western Australia in our first Shield game I made the players take advantage of the excellent Perth practice wickets in the afternoon which we had free. They knew they had to work and I spoke to the players individually, one of them Docking, our number six batsman, a good stroke-player who would lose concentration and try to hit out if he got bogged down. One of the ways of trying to stop him relaxing was to write on top of the blade of his bat the one word CONCENTRATION so he would see it every time he looked down to take guard. In a club game soon after we had been in Perth he scored a record 247 for his club, Yeoman, in the North West Association. That was the first year of Packer cricket so it was a little easier for us with so many top-class players being banned from the state teams.

Hampshire had an excellent season, scoring nearly 500 runs in the five Shield games for an average just under 50 and fully deserved his award as Tasmanian player of the season. Benneworth, overweight and struggling to diet, could have been a far better player, but he was keen, a great competitor and if we had entered the Shield a couple of years earlier I think he could have played for Australia. Cowmeadow, well-built, gutsy and determined, gave everything, and Docking was a great striker of the ball and a fine fielder anywhere. Doolan found it hard to open the batting and keep wicket and Howard — I had high regards for him — was a match-winner. Howard went to England to play in the Lancashire League with Nelson who were looking for a cheap professional. They wanted to pay £1,500 or £1,750 when others were paying £3,500 and I must say I was worried that being a professional in the Lancashire League might be too much for him on his first trip abroad. He started well but didn't keep it up the way the club expected and I think Nelson always blamed me, whereas the blame should have been where it belonged, with the club. I only scored 124 runs in the five Shield games, batting number seven or eight, and averaging just over 20. I bowled most overs but only picked up 11 wickets an an average of 39 which isn't very good. But I was pleased with a letter I saw from a spectator in Hobart, and spectators can be just as parochial as selectors and committee men, who said he wanted to pay tribute to Jack Simmons as captain of the Tasmanian team. "In my opinion," he wrote, "he has shown great qualities of leadership and has brought out the best in our players. The call of Old Trafford may still be strong but I believe he has an affection for Tasmania, too. It is possible to get good cricketers who are not leaders but in Jack Simmons we have a good cricketer who is also a great leader."

Tasmania had also had to sort out where to play their home games and unlike the other states there was no way we could have one centre. Some fools in Hobart, of course, thought

Tasmania couldn't play cricket anywhere other than Hobart. It really used to rile me when they talked like that for I believe it is good to spread the gospel of cricket, it was good we went to three different centres, Hobart, Launceston and Devonport, and the "gates" were extremely good at all of them. Another good point during this year was that there was no parochialism on the selection of teams — players were now picked purely on merit.

11
HOBART'S DAY OF HISTORY

By the time I returned to Tasmania for the 1978–79 season, their second in the Sheffield Shield, I had made up my mind that unless I was going to be paid by the Tasmania Cricket Council, I wasn't going to play for the state team. I felt very strongly about it. It wasn't the money at all, it was the pride of being a professional cricketer and that I'd been there seven years and played for nothing all the time, just like the amateurs. It was the principle of the matter — an offer of 1,000 or 2,000 dollars would thrill me to bits. Dennis Baker's wife hadn't settled as well as he had hoped and he told me he'd be looking for a substantial increase for 1978–79. Anyway, he didn't stay but went back to Western Australia and didn't play at all in our second season in the Shield, the last trial year before a decision was taken on whether we stayed in the competition. I arrived in Tasmania on Friday, 13 October, and was again met by the media who wanted to know how I thought Tasmania would fare in their second year in the Shield. I said I thought we could win one or even two matches and my biggest ambition was for Tasmania to win the Gillette Cup. I was more optimistic because players had improved the previous year. I had been asked at the end of the previous season whether I felt we should draw talent from other states and I said no. In earlier years it might have helped to have had a fast bowler, and perhaps another spinner to help me out would have been useful, but players were coming to the island of their own accord and I also thought we had a good batch of youngsters coming through.

I raised the question of money soon after I got there and after a good deal of haggling I was assured I would be paid for my games with Tasmania in the Sheffield Shield. No sum was mentioned at first and softie that I am, I agreed to play and captain Tasmania in what was to turn out to be my final year as a player with them. The N.T.C.A. promised they would get the money for me, they would guarantee it, and at the end of the season which was my best-ever for the state and was voted player of the season I received a bonus of 2,000 dollars. After my own personal performances with Lancashire in 1978 I was oozing with confidence, genuinely thinking Tasmania could go one better this season, win a Shield game and win the Gillette Cup. It was good to put this on record at the start of what did turn out to be Tasmania's best-ever season.

Our first game was in Adelaide, a beautiful city, a lovely ground with creeping ivy behind the main stand and close to the nets. A perfect place to start a season. I hadn't played there before and what I didn't realise was how long the ground was: a straight drive with the right fielder — maybe like yours truly — and the batsmen could run a six. Bob Blewett was again captain of the South Australia team and he was still saying ridiculous things to the Press such as his team were hoping to wrap up the game in three days. When the first day was washed out I couldn't resist telling the newspaper boys: "Well, now he's got his chance to prove it." Bruce Doolan, our wicketkeeper cum opening batsman from the previous season, had been dropped by the selectors from the twelve and Chris Hargreaves was brought in, a wicketkeeper, the selectors kept telling me, who was good, probably better than Doolan. We needed a number three batsman and although Hargreaves could bat there the selectors didn't want him to bat in that position but thought he should be blooded in the middle of the order, probably at number seven. But I thought: "Well, Simmo, you can't pick the side but there's one thing you do have the authority to decide on, the batting order." I had mentioned in the Press that if he got in the side there was a chance he would be at number three — the position he had played in the trials. I was probably being a bit hard on Hargreaves in his first match but I thought it would bolster our chances if I could revert Hampshire to the number four place. I was probably criticised but I thought why leave a good opening batsman — and keeper — out to replace him with a man I didn't think any better than Doolan as a wicketkeeper and definitely not as good a bat. So Hargreaves was thrown in at the deep end and scored 16 after the first wicket had fallen for 34.

From being 104 for two we had collapsed to 119 for six when I went in to bat, but I felt in good form and at the end of that opening day I was 74 not out. Norman stayed with me for quite some time and there was strong resistance the following day from the later batsmen, particularly Cowmeadow who helped me put on 61 runs in as many minutes. I still needed two for my century when the last man, Gary Whitney, came out, a former schoolboy opener but who had lost all touch as a batsman and had still to get off the mark that season. He shuffled forward to Sincock and pushed the first ball into the covers for a single and two balls later I lofted a ball wide of cover and took an easy two to get the century. Two overs later I was out but it had been a great moment for me, for not only had we recovered from a patchy start but I had recorded my first 100 in Australian first-class cricket. The first century of the season also earned 500 dollars from the Tasmania Cricket Council for the batsman, which went into the team pool. The same reward applied to the first bowler taking five wickets in an innings and I got that as well, along with two goblets which are now on my bar at home. Norman had taken nearly five hours to reach 50 and when Blewett was asked what he thought of the innings he said: "No comment." I defended his innings as the anchor man, as I thought it showed good temperament, but really the game seemed to become a battle of words with Blewett saying detrimental, stupid things like Tasmania were not trying to force a win and that he (Blewett) was the only captain trying to win. He seemed a Jekyll and Hyde character, making ridiculous remarks one minute and as nice as anything with you the next.

There is a tradition in Australian cricket that the teams go in each other's dressing room at the end of a day's play, depending on which team had been fielding. Rodney Hogg, the South Australian fast bowler who was not a Test player then, came to me on the first evening to ask if I had any tips for him, wanting to know how he had bowled. He was very accurate and I said I had one or two ideas I thought might help but I wasn't going to tell him until the end of the game. I would have looked a fool if he'd bowled us out after I'd given him advice! I told him I thought he sometimes bowled too straight, always attacking middle and off stumps and I didn't think he brought his slips into play often enough. The off-cutter was a stock ball but if a batsman was getting something just outside the off stump and nipping back he had to play and maybe bring the slips into action. We lost early wickets to Hogg in the second innings as it happened, but we still got a draw easily enough.

I have to confess I really was pleased with myself over that innings of 103 at Adelaide, only the third century I had scored in my career following 112 against Sussex at Hove in 1970 and 106 against Nottinghamshire at Old Trafford in 1978, just a few months before the one at Adelaide. It was quite a landmark for me, but an even bigger one was on the horizon in the Gillette Cup when we reached the final again after beating Queensland in the semi-final in another piece of last-over drama. Gary Goodman scored a century but David Boon, who was only eighteen years old, was the hero. Boon, playing his first match, had dropped down the order and was at the wicket with last man Gary Whitney when we went into the last over needing ten to win. Luckily Boon was on strike and after running a suicidal two, he hit two fours, one a marvellous hook, off Phil Carlson, to win us the match with only one ball to spare.

We played the semi-final in Brisbane and stayed there for a Sheffield Shield game which was to start five days later. The Gillette win gave a great lift to cricket throughout Tasmania and put us in good heart for the Shield game. After all, we had beaten a full Queensland side, so it had to give us confidence to take them on in the Shield without four Test players who were needed for Australia's game against India. To help fill in the time and hopefully give us good practice we played a South Queensland side and lost which probably did us a power of good, knocking that bit of cockiness out of us and bringing us back to reality.

We spent a couple of days free and it was good to be in

Brisbane with its beautiful weather and magnificent food. Some of us were invited to the home of the club doctor who had caught an enormous fish and which his wife cooked for us. It was delicious. And at the end of a day's play we used to wander twenty yards from the dressing room to a barbecue where wonderful T-bone steaks were served in lovely surroundings.

I hadn't played against South Queensland because of a nagging hamstring injury, but I returned for the state game in which we bowled Queensland out for 177 which allowed me to claim my career-best bowling return of seven for 59. I went on to bowl just before lunch and sent down 21 consecutive overs and saw them slip from 130 for two and lose those last eight wickets for 47 runs. There was a wind blowing in from fine leg and I really did bowl well. We let the chance of a good first innings lead slip through our fingers and in the end we were left to score 259 in 224 minutes which we hadn't much chance of making as their attack consisted entirely of seamers and we weren't going to get too many overs. We drew easily but it was disappointing again for me as I began to realise that no captain wanted to be the first to be beaten by Tasmania which I'm sure had a bearing on any team's declaration. Most of the time, if you put the opposition in to bat, you're hoping to make use of the early life in the wicket. But I must admit that with our bowlers, I didn't think we were capable of bowling any team out twice to win, but when batting last, with John Hampshire around, we always had a chance of chasing a target.

Our plans to fly out of Brisbane for Melbourne and then home were knocked back by an air strike involving the two domestic airlines, T.A.A. and Ansett, and there was every possibility of us being stranded in the Queensland capital over Christmas. We had already been away from home a week and there was no way we wanted that so I had a word with our manager about the chance of hiring aircraft. The following day we learned we had two chartered aircraft, one each for Hobart and Launceston. The one for Hobart left first, a six-seater with players and cases crushed together like sardines. I wasn't too bothered, I wasn't on that one, but on a rather bigger aircraft that took seven or eight of us. There was no hostess, nothing like that, just an esky with some beer and packets of biscuits. We had to go to Sydney to refuel and just before we got there we were faced with a huge black cloud, at about 10,000 feet. I thought I'd die if we hit that but because we were a small plane the pilot managed to get under it, though we were still shaken about a bit. We had trouble getting fuel and had to go in the country for it, flying by the coast and getting some fantastic views. We had left Brisbane just before lunch and it was midnight when we landed in Launceston. It was no highlight for me and I never want to go up again in a plane like that. The following day I had to present awards at three schools and though I couldn't have felt less like going anywhere I just had it to do. Then I went back to bed!

It was during our stay in Brisbane that we heard about the upheaval at Yorkshire over Geoff Boycott being sacked as captain, and the committee decision on who was to be the new captain. I was sharing a room with John Hampshire on that trip when he got a call from Joe Lister, the Yorkshire secretary, who said it had been decided to make him captain. Hampshire had never asked for the position and when he put the phone down he said to me: "That's the greatest honour I've ever been given." "But you've played for England," I said. "It doesn't matter," he said. "To be given the captaincy of the great Yorkshire club is the greatest thrill I've ever had." So we got champagne and a few beers and celebrated his appointment. It seemed funny to me that there was I, captain of Tasmania but never officially appointed captain of Lancashire, and there was John Hampshire, captain of Yorkshire but vice-captain to me in Tasmania. But we got on well together — we liked the same things and he has a great sense of humour — and if anything, it was going to make my job easier because he was more determined to get runs and prove a point to those Boycott fans who didn't want him.

It had been decided that the Gillette Cup final, again between Western Australia and Tasmania, would be held at Melbourne. It was a big disappointment to us all, particularly after we'd had to go to Perth for the previous year's final. It was said we couldn't play at Hobart because of television

MANCHESTER EVENING NEWS

£128,300! Receiving my benefit cheque in February 1981. With me are Jacqueline, Murray Birnie chairman of the benefit committee, my mother Ada, and Pat Birnie.

A moment of triumph! The 1984 Benson & Hedges Cup. This was my ninth Cup final, my sixth on the winning side.

Our wedding day in 1963.

Jacqueline and I walking in the streets of Lauceston, Tasmania.

Opposite page
Above *Jacqueline and I meet up with our old friend David Boon, Tasmania's Test batsman, at Headingley during Australia's 1985 tour of England.*

Below *With Jacqueline and our daughter Kelly.*

Above *Tasmania's first team to play in the Sheffield Shield, against Western Australia at Perth in 1977. Back row (from left): Mickey Norman, Stephen Howard, David Smith, Dennis Baker, Rowan Sherriff, Tony Benneworth, Garry Cowmeadow, Bruce Neill; front row: Trevor Docking, myself, Alan Carey (manager), Max Gillett (chairman), John Hampshire, and Bruce Doolan.*

Below *The captain leads his team in a different game, during a hold-up in Tasmania's first Sheffield Shield match. With me (from left) are Garry Cowmeadow, Trevor Docking, David Smith, Bruce Neill, and Bruce Doolan.*

Above *Kim Hughes c & b Simmons. A vital wicket in the 1979 Gillette Cup Final.*

Below *Leaving the field with Trevor Docking after sharing in a stand of 96 that took Tasmania to 180 for six.*

Victorious! Tasmania's Gillette Cup Final win over Western Australia in 1979.

ALL-SPORT PHOTOGRAPHIC

I had a marvellous bowling spell in the Benson & Hedges final of 1984. Who could think of retiring then?

ALL-SPORT PHOTOGRAPHIC

Cricket has given me a hell of a good life.

sponsorship commitments. But the whole thing seemed so unrealistic. Not many people would be travelling to Melbourne and I could just imagine ten people and a dog in that huge ground without any atmosphere at all. They also said they couldn't get television out of Tasmania. But then the Australian Cricket Board and Gillette got together, worked hard, contacted the television people in Hobart, and the decision was reversed with the game to be staged in Hobart which delighted us all, of course. It was a shot in the arm for Tasmania and it didn't matter which ground they'd have picked — it was bound to be packed.

The Launceston Bank for Savings, who had made a big contribution towards the sponsorship money needed to get me to return to Tasmania that season, had decided before the Brisbane semi-final that I should go on a meet-the-people campaign in Northern Tasmania for a week, coaching youngsters in bank foyers and even on the streets. The interest in cricket couldn't have been higher in Tasmania at that time and the Bank was able to take advantage of the publicity in the lead-up to the final. Sunday, 14 January 1979, was an historic day for Tasmania, for the island itself, not just for cricket. People asked me after how Tasmania had managed to beat Western Australia, the most professional side in Australia. I think we had improved a lot in twelve months and W.A. were not quite as good as before. But the biggest factor, I guess, had to be the fans. Their encouragement was colossal and none of our players were able to relax concentration and fielded brilliantly. We had picked a good side and the only criticism I had was in the choice of twelfth man, Mickey Norman, who was chosen for convenience and proved that cricket in Tasmania could still be amateurish. Norman was a dour player with few shots who had played some long, stubborn innings for the team in Shield matches but was not a good one-day player. He didn't have a strong arm, wasn't a particularly good fielder, and his little legs made him appear quicker than he actually was. He was chosen because his home was in Hobart and his selection saved a bit of money, a convenience choice rather than safeguarding against things going wrong. If someone had been hurt at practice the previous day, Norman still wouldn't have got into the side, so to me it was stupid to have him in the first place. But if somebody pulled out just before the start, then we would have been in trouble. Twelfth man should be chosen purely on form and money didn't really matter anyway because Gillette were paying the expenses.

The build-up for the match was enormous from television, radio and newspapers with special editions, and Cup Fever gripped Tasmania for a few days. I don't think too many of us slept as well as we would have liked the night before the match and we were all at the ground quite early. What a sight it was, driving up the hill overlooking the bridge and the bay with Mount Wellington over the other side and the area round the ground absolutely packed with cars and people. I must have been there one and a half to two hours before the game began and it was packed inside after many people had camped out all night in tents and queues had started to form at 6 a.m. to make sure of a prime place. If there were any Western Australia supporters there I never heard them!

I lost the toss again and John Inverarity put us in, just as he had done in 1977–78. Soon we looked to have no price of getting a respectable total as we crashed to 84 for six — and that after an opening half-century stand! Gary Goodman had scored 30, Stephen Howard 19, Tony Benneworth two, John Hampshire nine, Roger Woolley four, and David Boon eight and when I went in at the fall of the sixth wicket Trevor Docking was hanging on and had scored only a handful. It was rearguard action for a while and over the last five overs we gave it all we could, enabling us to at least reach 180 for six. That had been our plan and it had worked well with 66 runs coming in the last ten overs and while I'd thought before the game that 200 would give us a good chance of winning I was more than happy to get to 180 after being 84 for six. Docking scored 45 and I hit 55 not out in one of the best innings I've ever played with some backfoot shots over mid-wicket and square leg against a pretty good attack. The crowd was erupting, chanting, cheering us on and when we fielded we really were on our toes. Richie Benaud and Frank Tyson had gone through the W.A. side with me before the match and I had a little black book with all my notes on the various players. "Don't worry too much about Wood," they told me. "He'll run himself out." Wood and Inverarity opened the innings and started at a gallop with 39 runs very quickly. We had to try to curb the scoring rate and I put Docking at short mid-wicket, and sure enough Wood ran himself out due to a good pick-up and throw on the turn by Docking. It's not often you try to pressurise batsmen with close-in fieldsmen in a one-day game, but I did and was rewarded with a big turn-round as W.A. became 44 for three. Benneworth took three wickets in the middle of the order, Ric Charlesworth, Bruce Yardley and Kevin Wright, and had three for 18 in 8.2 overs when he fell and strained shoulder ligaments and had to go off. While Craig Serjeant was there I was a little worried and I badly wanted him out of the way when I came back for my last two overs. Only one run came off my first over and in my second, and last, Serjeant swept a ball to deep square leg where Mark Scholes took a catch in which the ball dropped out of his hands, then fell back in again on his chest. Everybody went doolally. We knew then they weren't capable of getting to our total. That was the end of my overs and I brought Cowmeadow back on from the same end and when he bowled Porter and the last man was caught behind we had won.

I was fielding at mid-off when the last wicket fell and there was an immediate invasion by the spectators. I couldn't stop jumping in the air, hitting my fist into space, and I ran off to the little pavilion where Jacqueline was sitting and hugged and kissed her. I could see Inverarity waiting to shake my hand but I'm afraid he had to wait. He said: "Very well played, Jack. You deserve your win." We all raced into the dressing room and I have never seen a side so excited. Every individual was still jumping about, the champagne and beer were out and the committee came in with big smiles on their faces. It was something they had probably never even dreamed about. The spectators were on the field in front of the pavilion and there appeared even more than at Lord's. They were chanting: "Simmo, Simmo," and it was a great feeling. Then we had to go on to the balcony where the chairman of Gillette presented the magnificent trophy for the last time — it was the last year of Gillette's sponsorship before McDonald's took over. When it was presented to me, I held it up and the roar was absolutely deafening. The Man of the Match award followed and I've never been so sure of getting the gold medal as I was then after scoring 55 not out, taking four for 17 and fielding like an eighteen-year-old. I was asked to say a few words — I said it was the greatest day of my cricketing life and what a great thrill it was. Tears were rolling down my cheeks, I was so overjoyed — a moment I'll never forget.

We celebrated in the dressing room for some time and the T.C.C., in their kindness, made a nice gesture in allowing us to stay overnight at their expense. A single room had been reserved for me anyway at Wrest Point for I was speaking at a Press lunch the following day but Jacqueline was staying now and I asked at reception if they would give me a double and I would pay the difference. The manager came out, said he wanted to congratulate me and not to worry about the room. It turned out to be a suite with a bar, kitchen, lounge and bathroom, absolutely lovely, with champagne and fruit with the compliments of the hotel. "Make the most of this," I thought. "It might not last much longer." We saved the champagne for another day and celebrated that night in the bar with the others, a great night that didn't finish until 4.30 a.m.

At about 8.30 I was wakened by the phone ringing. It was the Tasmanian Premier who wanted to add his congratulations and said I wouldn't realise the magnitude of interest our win would create. He said he felt the Government should help and asked me how much it would cost to send a youngster to England. Within half an hour somebody was at the hotel to discuss it, prepared, it seemed, to spend about 7,000 dollars. For somebody of nineteen or twenty it was a long way to go on his own so I decided to take the bull by the horns and suggested sending two. I said I thought they could do that for 10,000 dollars and I'd see it wasn't done on the cheap. I had to ring the Premier, Doug Law, who gave me his backing and said it would exist for five years. I know I was emotional the day before but this was marvellous news, to realise the Government was spending 50,000 dollars to send cricketers to England. He left it all to me to contact the Tasmania Cricket Council and to announce it at the Press Luncheon I was going to, an ideal way to get publicity. Kim Hughes had also agreed to speak at the lunch and he thought the Tasmanian idea was exceptionally good. Hughes impressed me that day with the way he handled the Press and I thought then he could well be the next captain of Western Australia, which is indeed what happened the following year when Inverarity went to Adelaide. Inverarity had applied for the headmaster's position at Launceston Grammar School and I couldn't have thought of anybody better to become Tasmanian captain as well. Unfortunately he didn't get the job and went to Adelaide instead where he did great work for South Australia.

The prize for winning the Gillette Cup was a game against England in Melbourne with 2,500 dollars for the winners and 1,500 for the losers. We were beaten there and then played England again at Launceston in a one-day match and at Hobart over three days. I met them at the airport and took them to the hotel and Ken Barrington, who was assistant manager, showed me their team, a full Test side apart from Mike Brearley who had stayed on the mainland. It was a great compliment to us but, of course, we lost again. Another England player who hadn't been able to go to Tasmania was Roger Tolchard, the reserve wicketkeeper, who had been injured during a match at Newcastle, just north of Sydney. David Bairstow was sent for to reinforce the side and he arrived in Tasmania while the England team were there. He was a good friend of both John Hampshire and myself and he ran in to Wrest Point, he was so happy to see us after an awful journey. The first thing he wanted to know was where the bar was so we could all have a drink together. It's always nice to meet somebody you like and respect and I felt we helped make his day on arriving.

Another first that Tasmania achieved that season was a victory in the Sheffield Shield, a truly satisfying win because it was against Western Australia again, the team that had won the Shield five times in the 1970s, including the previous two seasons. The game was at Devonport and the first person I always used to go to see there was Warren Squid, an apple grower and exporter. He had been a good player and had represented the north-west and worked hours and hours for Devonport, making sure the ground was properly prepared. The pitch had a slight tinge of green and I thought we might have a chance if we could get a few early batsmen out. But we didn't. They got a big score, we saved the follow-on and finished up with a day and a session in which to score 357, which had never before been scored for victory in a fourth innings. I dearly wanted to win because I was getting a lot of criticism at the time, some in the Press, some from committee and selectors, who thought I was going crackers, specially in putting W.A. into bat. They weren't as friendly as usual to me during the game and I had to confess they were possibly right up to a point.

The reason I had put them into bat was that I had been told the wicket would stay good for four days and as it always got low and slow our best chance of victory always seemed to be in hoping for a reasonable declaration. Perhaps Inverarity thought we had no chance of getting 357 after struggling our way through the first innings. The one good thing about his declaration was that at least we had a long time to bat, no need to be chasing the clock all the time. On a wicket that wasn't doing too much I thought we had an outside chance so I got the players together before we started and said: "Never think about the total of 357. We'll set a target for each session and that's all I want you to have in your mind." We also had to conserve wickets and we laid down targets, something like 75 for one at the end of that day's play, leaving us about 280 to get on the last full day. Then we set targets for lunch and tea and while we managed to keep up with them as far as runs were concerned we had lost more wickets than I wanted. When I went in between lunch and tea we needed 172 with four wickets standing. It looked hopeless but I had set out to win that game, luck seemed to be with us and Roger Woolley was playing well. His concentration was good although he played the occasional rash shot and I kept going down the wicket to talk to him. "We can win this game if you stay there," I told him. "But if you play rash shots you're going to get out and I can't imagine anyone else getting the runs we need." There weren't too many people there at the start of play but as the day progressed and we got nearer victory more kept coming in especially after the tea interval. Once we got to the last hour we wanted just over 80 and victory was in sight. I was determined to keep going for the first-ever Shield win for Tasmania which we achieved after a partnership of 172. Inverarity and his players applauded us off the field, shook my hand and congratulated us. We had had luck with a few iffy shots close to fielders, but that's the way the game goes.

It was a great thrill and a lot of pressure went off the players. I think a lot went off the other states as well, now they weren't going to be the first to lose to Tasmania. There were more photographs in the dressing room and I don't think I've ever felt as tired after a game, not because of the overs I'd bowled or the time I batted, but just the sheer concentration plus the pressure from the criticism I'd been getting. The following day it was headlines again, "Tassie re-born," and the state reception we had been promised for winning our first Shield game was on the way. By this time it had been announced that I was receiving a benefit in England in 1980 and wouldn't be returning the following year, and the reception in many ways was like a farewell to me. The Premier phoned, said they were inviting 300 guests to the function to be held in Launceston and wanted to know who I would like to be there before any other invitations were sent out. I felt honoured and I asked for Mr and Mrs Donaldson, who had been like a second father and mother to us, to Elizabeth and Udo who we had stayed with, a few other friends, some of them who weren't cricket nuts. It was a tremendous occasion with all the Members of Parliament and Government officials there and a big surprise was the presentation of a big silver salver made to me, "in appreciation of unprecedented work to cricket and coaching in Tasmania," with a decanter and cut-glass wine glasses. These were all to be sent through the diplomatic bag to Tasmania House in the Strand in London. I'm not the best of speakers by any means and although I had a few notes with the names of people I wanted to thank I just kept choking up and finally had to stop.

There were no tears for the T.C.C., a few for friends in the N.T.C.A., but mostly they were for friends not connected with cricket, those who had looked after us. All the players were there and we were all presented with cufflinks, with the Tasmanian crest, by the Premier. It turned out to be just one hell of a fantastic night, very emotional.

The Bank and some friends who were not on the N.T.C.A. committee, said they would stage a benefit match for me, a starter for my benefit in England. Tony Benneworth, the promotions man for the Bank, and David McQuestin, general manager of the television station TNT 9, were among those involved and contacted players from various states including Allan Border, Graeme Wood, Bruce Yardley and Graham Yallop, all of whom were sponsored and paid a small fee. What really tickled me was that the occasion was commemorated with a bottle of port, a label being struck with Jack Simmons port which was sold out within days. They saved me a case and the Government even allowed that to go to London through the diplomatic bag so I wouldn't have to pay custom duty. Unfortunately I did have to pay duty when it arrived, about £30 for the case. I wasn't too bothered as I knew it would be good for the benefit. The match raised 19,000 dollars from about 7,000 people and in the end I was given a cheque for 12,000 dollars, which was a wonderful effort. I know the big sponsors, the Bank, television and the airline, had put in sizeable donations but I felt the money had come from the people of Tasmania, moreso the kids, who had all been given a day off from school to attend the game.

The Launceston ground had always had the same caterers on match days but on this occasion a man called Ron Merritt and his wife Mavis, catered for everyone. Ron had a pub at Mole Creek, thirty or forty miles away, and his contribution, rather than put in money, was to cater for everyone who was having lunch — players, administrators and guests. He put on a fantastic menu, including fresh lobster, and the usual forty-minute lunch break had to be extended in order to appreciate the meal properly. It must have cost him an absolute fortune to put it on, prepare it and get staff to serve it.

He had once rung the N.T.C.A. to ask if I would go to Mole Creek where they had one school for infants, juniors and seniors. We couldn't get him into the itinerary for the coaching programme so I said I would go when I had finished at Westbury which meant I wouldn't have to travel so far, maybe another fifteen miles. I conducted the coaching after school with about forty youngsters varying from five years old to nineteen. We only had a concrete pitch without any nets but we coped as well as we could and everybody seemed pleased. Before I was allowed to do any coaching I had to go to Ron's pub and have a meal, salmon, the likes of which I've never tasted before or since. Absolutely superb. He insisted that when I finished I had to go back to the pub but halfway through the coaching he appeared with ice cream and a soft drink for every youngster. When I had arrived at the school playing field there had been a brand new set of equipment for all the kids, a generous gesture from a generous man. When I returned to the pub I had a few drinks and was introduced to all his customers before he said I must have something more to eat, maybe a T-bone steak, because I hadn't eaten all the fish. That salmon was a monster, but I did manage to eat the other half before the pub closed about 10.30 p.m. when I said I would have to be going. I had been talking to members of the cricket team, answering questions, putting over a few points, and when we got outside he asked me how much I wanted. I said nothing but he insisted on giving me twenty dollars for petrol and brought out two jars of honey, a rabbit, eggs and a trout. I couldn't help smiling, it was like the old days when you paid in food and goods before money. Ron called everybody "bloke". "How are you going on, bloke?" He had a big nose as if it had been stung with bees but it isn't the looks of a fellow you go on, it's what's behind the face and Ron was one of, if not the, nicest blokes I've ever met. I believe he put 500 dollars into the appeal to bring me back. We all became very good friends and after one game at Devonport the team called in for a meal at his request. Jacqueline and I and Tony Benneworth and his wife decided to stay the night and the following morning we got up early, had breakfast of double eggs, bacon, sausage and steak, and then were shown his young farm animals. Then he said: "Just look at that!" and there, on one of the fence posts, was a big silver salver with a bottle of champagne and six glasses and we had to have a drink before we were allowed to leave. He just kept saying: "Why take it with you? I'm going to enjoy it and see enjoyment from it." All the lads appreciated him and nobody went to Ron for what they could get, they went in sincerity and wanted to chat to him. He was a generous man and laid on all the wine, too, at the benefit match lunch.

The 12,000 dollars from the benefit match were put in an account for me in the Launceston Bank for Savings and when I was back home in England a letter arrived to say I would be taxed to the tune of 5,000 dollars. I wrote to Tom Room and told him what applied in England. We had not traded, the books were seen, and after a few months of lobbying the matter was dropped although I'd had to pay the 5,000 dollars, and then claim it back.

I stayed in England for the next two winters and helped arrange for Brian Davison, the Southern Rhodesia batsman who was with Leicestershire, to go out there. He became captain and the Tasmanian team continued to improve. I was always interested to hear how the players were progressing, particularly David Boon who I had known from my earliest years. Two years really zipped by as I concentrated on my benefit in England and then Tasmania wrote to me. Would I like to go back and coach, and was I interested in playing. I thought I would like to play and be paid a little bit but I knew I couldn't emulate what I'd done in the previous two years and it would be better to go out remembered for those years rather than play again, get paid and not do so well. So I said no. I had had a couple of successful seasons with Lancashire with over 1,000 runs in all competitions in 1980 and a fairly good year in 1981 so there was a bit of life in the old dog, now forty years old. But thinking of Tasmania as much as myself it was better to say no. What they really needed was a good fast bowler and so when I returned to Tasmania later I got Franklyn Stephenson for them, a West Indian fast bowler I had seen bowling in England. He was quick and while he had never before played a first-class game I felt he could be of service to Tasmania. I knew I was taking a bit of a gamble but luckily we were attached to the same club at Mowbray and he started in great fashion, quick and fiery and taking wickets, glaring at the batsmen in good Aussie fashion. He tended to get upset with the umpires who would no-ball him for breaking the return crease and on a couple of occasions I had to talk to him, nicely at first, then put my foot down. But he responded and we went on to win the league for the first time ever in 1981–82. He made a great start for Tasmania, taking ten wickets in his first match, at Melbourne, which helped them win by 96 runs, their first win on the mainland in five years in the Shield. *Wisden* described Stephenson as impressive in the first innings, when he took four for 27, and often unplayable in the second, when he had six for 19. He went on to take 36 wickets for Tasmania, a Shield record for them, and finished second in the national averages, but, as often happens, he killed the goose that was laying the golden egg. He had been offered a contract of 10,000 to 12,000 dollars to promote soft drinks and tried to cash in on his season by asking Tasmania for double his salary for 1982–83. Tasmania hadn't that sort of money and he went home to Barbados because of family illness. Because he had done so well he expected so much, but asked for too much. Instead, he signed as one of the West Indian rebels for South Africa and I later helped him play for Gloucestershire. I told him once I wished I'd had his ability. If I had I would have played for England. And I meant that.

Davison missed the following season because of his benefit at Leicestershire but Tasmania had two West Indians in Roland Butcher, the Middlesex batsman, and fast bowler Michael Holding, two thorough gentlemen who made a great impression. Butcher scored only one half century which was disappointing, but Holding, as everybody expected, bowled well as Tasmania became a full member of the Shield for the first time and played a full ten matches instead of five. Neil Williams, the Middlesex pace bowler, went over in 1983–84 and the following year saw another new face in Patrick Patterson, the West Indian fast bowler who had signed for Lancashire. I didn't know anything about Patterson's character or personality and his quietness perhaps made him hard work for the sponsors who really need somebody with an outgoing personality. Patterson had problems in Tasmania because he was on his own, there was nobody he knew, nobody, it seemed, to turn to, and he had a dispute with the Tasmanian captain, now Roger Woolley, which finished with a series of bouncers at Woolley in the nets. So Patterson was dropped in what turned out to be an unhappy season for him.

The enjoyable part of going back to Tasmania in those seasons from 1981–84 and deciding not to play was that I was then offered a job as one of the television commentators, something that kept me in touch with the game and the players and which I thoroughly enjoyed. Not that it was easy. I had great difficulty at first trying to concentrate on the game and still have somebody talking to me through the ear piece, and I also found it hard to watch the play on a monitor set instead of seeing it live. After all, if you watch live, you could start to talk about something the viewer couldn't see which would be annoying. On one occasion the producer was bawling "Four, four" in my ear when the ball had only gone for two. But it was camera four he was referring to. A few letters of complaint arrived from people who objected to my bias towards Tasmania when commentating. My co-commentator Neville Oliver, said I would have to get used to not saying "Us" when I was talking about Tasmania. But how could I help it? I *was* biased and I said if you think I'm biased in saying I hope Tasmania get an early breakthrough or score quick runs, then you're quite right. I've never had a great command of the English language and I had to write down words I thought I'd like to use. It was great fun for me, although not always the best of conditions and absolutely freezing at times. Don Closs, head of A.B.C. sport in Hobart, was excellent, I suppose on other sports, but technical points in describing cricket let him down. Such remarks as: "Well, that was a beautiful slips drive" or "Why is leg slip so deep?" when he should have been referring to fine leg.

I did three years coaching and commentating in Tasmania between 1981 and 1984 and when I arrived for my last season in

October 1983, I was met by chairman Jack Bennett, and secretary Cedric Knight who said they were sorry, but in order to provide money for me, they'd had to take on extra sponsors. "We've actually sold your soul," Jack Bennett said to me. As well as the schools I normally did, I had been sub-let to a club, Old Scotch, as coach-captain. I said I didn't mind that. "We've also got sponsorship from the grammar school through two young business friends of mine," which was a separate arrangement because it was a private school. So in addition I had to go into a sports shop on a Saturday morning which disappointed me because it was the only morning I could lie in. It was a complete change which I didn't mind, but on occasions my day was running from 9.15 a.m. to 10.30 p.m. with coaching and selecting teams. I was completely exhausted when I got home, and that year became very hard. So I can understand Old Scotch being a little disappointed at me for not being as keen as they expected. I gave Old Scotch everything when we played though and I bowled a lot of overs. We weren't that good a side but we were a happy team and we did win a few games. James Whittaker, from Leicestershire, had gone over with me and proved to be a great asset to the club, a good, young, attacking batsman. But that year, with all the hard work and the sponsorship deals, I was feeling very tired by Christmas and was forever falling asleep in the chair at home. This was affecting Jacqueline and our daughter, Kelly, so we talked it over and decided it would probably be our last year. I was sad at the thought because we had had ten wonderful years in Tasmania and it wouldn't seem the same, not looking forward to our winters there. I enjoyed Old Scotch, a good club right from the top, from chairman David Chugg, and they were excellent people, but I couldn't give everything to the two practice nights.

In all those years there was only one club I didn't enjoy playing with and that was Westbury where Bob Ingamells was Mister Cricket although he wasn't an official in my year. My first experience of the place was to find that an official who was due to welcome me at my first practice at the club didn't arrive because he was in custody for being drunk and disorderly.

Other incidents happened through the year that stopped us being a happy side and the club hadn't a good reputation. I wasn't happy at the club and I didn't do to well at Westbury, the only club I was attached to that didn't make the finals.

Games were played over two Saturdays in the N.T.C.A. and if the wicket wasn't too bad and you won the toss you would always bat first. If you didn't and they got 200 or 300 Heaven knows what the wicket would be like the following week. I once played at Westbury over a Saturday-Monday, the long weekend, with an outfield that was quite long on the Saturday. We batted and got a good score and as I was afraid the ground might be cut, I asked the umpires if they would not only inspect the wicket but the outfield to make sure it was in a reasonable and similar condition. On the Monday I pointed out that the outfield had been cut short ready for them to bat. It was denied, of course, but there were piles of grass cuttings on the bike track surrounding the ground. It was just a matter of their word against yours. On another occasion, before I went there, during a long spell of beautiful weather when it hadn't rained a drop in Launceston through the week between innings, the wicket for the visitors to bat second on was wet from batting crease to batting crease. They simply said there had been a local shower. It was so localised that it wasn't wet on the run-ups and it wasn't wet at the delivery stride — just wet on the wicket itself! It was laughable. At other times, I heard, there would be two pitches, one prepared, the other uncut and looking as if it was for the kids, very, very grassy and if the visitors won the toss, looked at the wicket and decided to bat, by the time they got out there, the stumps were in the other wicket! Unfortunately, Westbury became the club every other side wanted to beat and players have left them to go into Launceston to join other clubs. Many were afraid of moving for they thought if they did, they would have little chance of playing for the N.T.C.A. or Tasmania. I've got on with Bob Ingamells and I've disliked him but I've admired him and had to acknowledge that the amount of time he gave to cricket was enormous. He was always up at 6 a.m., as many do in Australia, and would go and roll the Westbury wicket. His wicket preparation and organisation of youngsters had to be admired. But he was a love-hate fellow, admired because of his hard work but not really liked. He so hated to lose that some youngsters became afraid of him, but then he would put eleven kids in his car so they wouldn't have to pay the bus fares to the ground. He would do anything, but wanted 150 per cent on the field and some boys would be frightened of failure. A dropped catch, a misfield, a bad shot or a bad ball and the kid would shiver a little bit. But it could also bring out the best in one or two, enough to turn a competition.

We thought it would be our last year in 1983–84 but I still tried to arrange a programme in which I would not be attached to a club and would do the bulk of the coaching to end just before Christmas when Jacqueline and Kelly would fly out for a month and then return. I was at the point where I thought I could have done it for the money they were going to receive from the education authorities when I received a letter from John Goodsall who had been assistant head at one of the schools, saying he was sorry to hear I wouldn't be returning as coach to the N.T.C.A., that they had got someone from Sydney and thanked me for all the work I had done with the youngsters. It disappointed me that I hadn't been told by the N.T.C.A. and I couldn't help thinking about loyalties. People had been asking me whether I was going back to Tasmania and I had been saying I hadn't made up my mind. Well, that had made up my mind for me. A sad way to end a ten-year association.

And to think, there had been a time when I thought our future might lie in Tasmania. I never knew how long I would be playing at Lancashire and with the success we had had in Tasmania there was always the chance of settling there. Jacqueline wasn't keen but we would have had to consider it if I was offered the position of state coach or, as it is now, state director of coaching, or some other post. It wasn't offered but I did apply for the manager's job when I finished playing and I got a nice reply saying they felt they couldn't accept me as I couldn't be there to take pre-season training or winter nets. But in only my second or third year there I was so attached to Tasmania and felt so strongly that there might be a future in coaching or administration for me, that I bought land

Launceston. I had problems transferring money from England to Australia but there are always ways. Tony Benneworth, the Tasmanian player, was professional with Lowerhouse in the Lancashire League and when he ran out of money I lent him some and his father put the same amount into my account in Tasmania. Within two years the land was mine and I did intend building a house there, a nice area of Launceston, quiet, close to the city and the club. That gave me an idea to build an indoor cricket school at the Launceston ground, so I drew up the plans and got Cedric Knight, the N.T.C.A. secretary, as a partner so that he'd arrange the bookings, and I'd do the coaching. It was going to cost me £25,000 and was to be another encouragement for going there to live. The N.T.C.A. agreed not to charge me rent or rates for the first two years, then they would take a percentage of the profits we made and I was delighted with the whole venture. The following summer, when I was back in England, I received a letter to say the cricket school was going ahead with government backing. There was nothing I could do. There was nothing in writing and what would have been a profitable commercial enterprise was lost. I was quite upset, especially in following years when it became something of a dump. It was cleaned up from time to time but it could have been improved, it could have been maintained better.

We had many wonderful, satisfying years in Tasmania, and made lots of marvellous friends. The really nice part was the friends that Jacqueline made with the players' wives, particularly the Donaldsons, Marie, Colleen, Jill, Denise, Vicky Knight, Fran Jacobson, Lynn Farrell and others who stayed good friends through our years there. And in our last two seasons there, through coaching at the private school, Jacqueline, our daughter Kelly and I became good friends of Gordon and Judy Humphreys, Bill and Sue Woolcock, Clive and Jenny Hill, Mike and Robin Courtenay, and their families. We were good friends, too, of Jack and Shirley Bennett but Cedric Knight, for so long secretary to the N.T.C.A., was my best mate. He came to this country once and stayed ten weeks, travelling round with Lancashire and was even our twelfth man at Portsmouth. He said it was the best ten weeks of his life beautifully climaxed with the presentation to him by our chairman, Cedric Rhoades, of a Lancashire crest, which he treasures. So to end with Tasmania was sad.

12
£128,300!

During my season in Tasmania in 1978–79 I received a letter from the Lancashire chairman, Cedric Rhoades, to tell me that the committee had decided to give me a benefit in 1980. The chairman knew I had been to Tasmania many times and enjoyed it and that if he waited until I returned to England before telling me, I would probably have already signed another contract for the next Australian season. Tom Room, the Northern Tasmania Cricket Association chairman, was a good friend of Cedric Rhoades and there was no way Lancashire or I wanted to let Tasmania down. So I was given plenty of advance warning which allowed me to tell the N.T.C.A. I wouldn't be returning for the next two winters, 1979–80 and 1980–81 while I concentrated on the benefit. Lancashire also told me that my contract, which was due to come up for renewal at the end of the 1979 season, had already been extended for another year. I was surprised to get a benefit ahead of David Hughes who had been capped a year before me but I thought their decision was based as much on age as anything, that they thought Hughes, who is six years younger than me, would be around Old Trafford a lot longer.

The early notice gave me plenty of time to get organised, to order bats, collect them, have them signed, time to think who I would like on the committee and in particular who would be number one man and run the show. When I returned to England in 1979, Barry Wood was only a third of the way through his benefit year and there was no way I could take his committee members and interfere with his organisation. Murray Birnie, a friend who had been involved in the benefits for Farokh Engineer and Clive Lloyd and had been chairman of David Lloyd's committee, was the man I wanted. David Lloyd had raised £40,000 through excellent organisation in 1978 and I was delighted when Murray, after talking it over with his wife, Pat, agreed to run mine as well. We then had to form a committee and to start with a vice-chairman. We asked Bill Griffiths who had worked in previous benefits, was efficient and meticulous, and was in charge of all ground functions, raffles and collections. Bill was well organised, didn't want to be part of anything slipshod, and didn't have time for inefficient people who couldn't do a job the way he wanted. He was an enthusiastic Lancashire member and I think he was delighted to be a part. Both Murray and I wanted some friends on the committee so we went through various regulars at Old Trafford. He involved big Neville Neville who became the social secretary, which was just up his street, and I wanted Frank Greenwood, my bank manager, to be treasurer. I didn't have all that much money in the NatWest then, but we still got on well! NatWest gave him permission and that was their contribution, but as money came in we put it into Building Societies to earn interest and attract sponsorship.

When you form a committee you have to be careful you have people with the right principles but first and foremost, they have to want to work for the beneficiary and they have to be honest. It has been known in some benefits for money not to find its way into the beneficiary's fund. Another man I wanted was an old mate I had known since I was a youngster at Enfield Cricket Club, Mick Hill. When we both worked for Accrington Brick and Tile, Mick ran a little pool for the Catholics, a shilling a week, and prizes of a few pounds. I would give Mick various amounts, get in front sometimes, behind at others and at one period I hadn't been to where he worked in the electricians' shop and had got four or five weeks behind. Many agents would have cut me off. I hadn't paid so I wasn't involved. Mick didn't do that, but put the money in himself and when my number came up for first prize after about six weeks he handed over the money — about £10 which was a lot for a sixteen-year-old in 1957. That was honesty. He needn't have told me, he could justifiably have said I hadn't contributed for too long and, as we joined on tickets then, kept the money himself. Mick was a bachelor with his own business and became my right-hand man — my minder, you could say. If I had too much to drink at functions he would drive me home although we usually took it in turns. He was in charge of the bats, getting them to me, and organising me to get them signed.

Our first committee meeting was held in September at the end of the 1979 season and Roy Wilkinson, who had just got on the board of Matthew Brown, said he thought the brewery should be involved in a benefit for a local boy and asked if I would accept a car with their name, and mine, on it for the benefit year. They also got involved in other ways so we decided to use the Trafalgar, a Matthew Brown hotel, near Preston and close to the M6 motorway, for our meetings. One of my biggest worries was that the four previous beneficiaries at Lancashire, Barry Wood, David Lloyd, Clive Lloyd and Farokh Engineer, had all been Test players with contacts through the international arena. They had got good prizes, partly through those contacts, and I wondered whoever was going to give me anything like that. Clive had had a holiday for two in the West Indies donated, a super prize that was auctioned at a big function at the Piccadilly Hotel in Manchester. I thought — who the heck's going to give me a holiday? And that made me nervous, wondering whether I could get worthwhile prizes for the various functions throughout the year. During our first meeting, I nearly dropped through the floor when Murray said 800 prizes would have to be found at no cost to the benefit fund. Eight hundred! Where were we going to get that number from? He said it didn't matter what they were: bottle of after-shave somebody didn't want, that tin of talc Uncle Bill had got for Christmas and was still sitting on the shelf unopened, anything, just anything the committee could come up with! Murray organised many of the prizes and even before the benefit was underway they started to roll in. Go to Phillips, he said, and they handed over a box full of small appliances like razors and toasters. We did get holidays too, and good holidays; we received a holiday to Barbados from Don Chivers of Sun

Living, another from Caribbean Connection, and a holiday in Torremelinos for two weeks, through Chris Hassell, the Lancashire secretary. What made me feel humble was the help I got from members, my sisters Vera and Betty and Jacqueline's family who all wanted to assist in their own way. Gladys and Norman Jobson asked if I would like some soft toys, something for Gladys to do and enabled her to take part. She arrived early in December with a box full of them including a big Paddington Bear, about two feet high, that must have cost them quite a bit of money. John Parkinson couldn't get involved because of his business but he helped get contacts for the brochure, the brewery provided prizes, like crates of vodka, and I was flabbergasted at the help I got, particularly from members who just wanted to do their bit.

In those days we lived in Ash Lane in Great Harwood, a small two-bedroomed bungalow, and as the prizes started to pour in, it got to the point where we had so many that we bought another house to accommodate them. Well — not just for that reason, but it was good to have the room for the prizes, bats, pontoon jars, and everything else we needed. Another major item was the brochure and its advertising which had to be organised before the benefit started and Murray and I had a private little bet about who would get most adverts. It created competitiveness and the brochure, which I thought was a handsome production, was sorted out well in advance. A lot of work went into deciding who we should ask to contribute articles to the brochure and I don't think I had a refusal from anybody I asked. I had always got on with Peter West, the television commentator, and he responded quickly with an article. I wrote to thank him for his promptness in obliging and back came another letter to say it was the first time he had ever been thanked for contributing an article. When the brochures were printed I sent him a couple of copies and again he wrote back to thank me for my courtesy in sending them, again the first he had had. It was lovely. People like Jim Laker, Clyde Walcott, my hero, Bob Paisley, Clive Lloyd, John Arlott, Mike Brearley, Dickie Bird, Brian Johnston, Ken Barrington, Frank Tyson all contributed. So, too, did Fred Trueman who said:

"I'll always help fellow cricketers, but you Jack, I'll help twice." He contributed an article and also spoke at two or three dinners for me.

When it was announced that I was to have a benefit I received lots of letters from clubs offering to stage matches. The beneficiary only gets so many free days in a season and we couldn't possible have held matches at all the clubs who had asked. We had a cricket match committee and we then had to work out which ones we thought would be most beneficial, which we could select without hurting anybody's feelings. Murray wasn't too keen on going to Enfield but I said I didn't care if we didn't make a penny, I was going. It was my home club, it was where I'd been brought up, where my father and grandfather had played and no matter what happened, a match had to be played there. I had my favourites, Murray had his, and working from his computer brain of pounds, shillings and pence, we managed to sort them out. We told clubs we hadn't enough free dates to arrange matches for them all but we would go along for a dinner, a potato pie supper, a sports forum, or whatever they suggested. None of the clubs that asked was refused and in the end we went to over 100 of them in the year. This is a way, I feel, to put something back into the game at grass roots level when you have a benefit match involving the county side. Obviously, the beneficiary is the main reason the game is being held but clubs, although they have a lot of hard work, can make money at the bar, through catering and car park, and the publicity is good for everybody.

Right at the end of the 1979 season I was at the bar at the Grand Hotel, Leicester, having a drink with our dear old scorer, Mac Taylor, and Clive Lloyd. Mac said he wanted to see me get a good benefit then he would retire as all his best mates would then have had benefits. I said to Clive: "You're going to be a good mate, aren't you? I played in every game for you, clothed you, ran you about, acted like a minder to you. Yet you won't be able to do a thing for me, you'll be on tour in the winter, come back here and tour England with the West Indies, then you'll be off to Australia. A good mate you're proving to be. Anyway, it's your round. Three gin and tonics." Clive got the drinks and said: "You're right. I won't be able to help much." I said I was only joking. If he could find time to nip in for a pre-season game before the West Indies arrived and if he could maybe speak at a dinner, I'd be grateful. He told me to look at the fixtures for Lancashire and the West Indies and if there was a vacant day and they were anywhere nearby, they'd come up and play a game for me. I said to him: "You'll come up?" He said no, "I'll bring the West Indies up." I thought that was a great gesture, a real opportunity so I reported this to Murray who was in charge of my diary. We discovered that after the West Indies had played Yorkshire at Headingley they had Tuesday off before arriving on the Wednesday for the next Test at the Oval. I told Clive we also had that Tuesday off and he agreed to take his side to Blackpool for a match. We were given an anonymous £2,000 donation which had to be split between the club and the beneficiary and around 7,000 people saw the game. We had quite a few expenses, but every West Indies player played for nothing. We went to Leeds to pick them up, put them in a hotel and hired a coach to take them to London, but it still proved to be one of the biggest returns on a benefit match I've ever heard of with Blackpool handing me a cheque for £4,000. John Jallal, who owns the Town and Country Restaurant in Blackpool, a man I had known for years, provided all the food for the West Indies with champagne and wine for the coach journey and also provided the Man of the Match award.

A benefit year runs strictly from 1 January to 31 December and while I didn't start right on the dot of New Year's Day I was out the following day to see if pubs would take pontoon jars. I took six that day and took more every lunchtime and evening when I didn't have a function. In all I went to 810 pubs with the jars which raised me a lot of money. When Barry Wood left the club soon after getting his benefit cheque of £63,000 it hit me hard for quite a while. People were stopping me to say: "And I suppose you'll clear off at the end of the season as well," and within two weeks of Wood leaving three dinners were cancelled. The occasional landlord reacted like that for a week or two but it didn't last. There was a meeting at my house every

Saturday morning when Murray would write out my diary for the week with every function, lunchtime meeting, cricket match, and if I hadn't anything on I went out every lunchtime and evening with the jars. We had a lot of help with them: one member, Tom Ashcroft, took them round — and they were the size of toffee jars — by bus to the pubs of Warrington. They were a good source of income, as the tickets provided an immediate prize. We did have one hiccup towards the end of the year with the jars when we were persuaded to order 100 more for which we paid £2,000 and which we didn't sell. But that was our only mishap.

By the time the season started I was getting used to late nights and had to adopt a safety method of going out and drinking. I never liked soft, fizzy drinks, they blew me up just as much as beer, so I went on dry martini and tonics, a long drink with plenty of ice which never seemed to affect me. I never once felt I was incapable of driving or would come out on the wrong side of a breathalyser. I was stopped a couple of times by the police for speeding during the winter and they were kind to me. "On another benefit do, Jack?" they'd say. "Well, just be careful going through the town. It's a thirty zone." A friend got me a breathalyser and I would test myself having had say, five of the dry martini and tonics, even ten or twelve, and be all right. I was still at some functions after midnight and I tried various ways with the drink, with and without food, and never once was I over the limit with my breathalyser.

Pure delegation and organisation made my benefit the success it was. Murray Birnie and the committee thought I was a good selling commodity, popular in the leagues I had played in, and Murray wanted to capitalise on that popularity. But everything we did, we wanted to give value for money. Every committee meeting we had, seemed to be a pleasure for everyone and I never felt any friction. People got closer and more friendly and it was enjoyable from the first meeting, right through the hard times. There were nearly thirty people on the committee but only one fell by the wayside which I think says a lot for the feeling of the members. In the early stages of a year everybody is keen and wants to take part but with these people it persisted throughout the year and I'm eternally grateful to them all. Murray instilled in me that I had to give 100 per cent all the time. Other players, I know, felt that once they were into their benefit it couldn't be taken away and if they slipped into the second team that was to their advantage, giving them more time to concentrate on their benefit. Murray never believed that and impressed on me, the better you do, the more publicity and popularity you attract. I found it a bit hard to believe at first but it didn't make any difference, I always did as I was told. Through the summer we eased off on functions and concentrated more on cricket because Murray wanted all my time and effort devoted to Lancashire County Cricket Club as a member of the side.

Up to 1 July I was allowed to look at the bank balances, and up to then there was little on the plus side. For one thing we had got 1,980 pontoon jars which had cost us nearly £35,000. After July finance was never discussed so it would be a surprise to the beneficiary and by tradition with Lancashire benefits the figure had to be stated publicly at the same time. So believe me, the supporters, the people who had contributed so handsomely, knew the the final figure at the same time as I did. Well, within a few hours. I know many people thought I was pulling the wool over their eyes when I said I didn't know the figure and right at the end I really had no idea except that it had gone successfully. Only three people knew how it was going — Murray, Bill Griffiths and the treasurer Frank Greenwood. I would go in the bank as a customer and talk about the benefit but Frank never betrayed that secret. It was kept a secret and I wasn't told, although I tried to find out once or twice. Towards the end of the year the club secretary, Chris Hassell, went to a question and answer function and was asked how my benefit was going. He said it was a tremendous success and when asked if it had beaten Barry Wood's, he said he was sure it had. Could it make six figures, somebody asked. He said he wouldn't be surprised if it did and the headline in the local paper the following day referred to Simmons making a £100,000 benefit. I was a bit annoyed when I heard about it to think somebody else knew when I didn't. So I rang Murray who told me it was a load of rubbish. "They're way out, Jack, twenty odd thousand out." So I thought from that I would be making £25,000 less, not more. Say £75,000.

On the night, when everybody expected Murray to hand over the cheque he gave it to Mick Hill, my right-hand man and chauffeur, minder, companion and friend, to present it to me — a huge cheque, three feet by two feet with photos of the committee round it. The first I knew of the final figure was when Murray mentioned it in his speech — £128,300. I was speechless and I was glad Murray carried on speaking because I couldn't have composed myself to have replied. It was a great occasion with over 300 people there, family as well as friends including my mother who was in a wheelchair and had been brought by ambulance. I got through the speech, which was written out, but I was amazed I did. From that point on, not just my life was secure but that of my wife and probably anybody connected with our families if any problems arose.

That was a marvellous night and the following morning Murray arrived at the house with the pass books for all the buildings societies and the bank books, all to be signed over to me. "It's all yours now," said Murray. "It's your responsibility." Murray and I were due in Blackburn that morning for a radio broadcast and as we were leaving, because Murray was staying to lunch, Jacqueline asked me to get some bacon on the way home. I was still in a bit of a whirl but I managed to remember to stop and get 2lb of bacon but when I came to pay I hadn't a penny in my pocket. I felt terrible, but I had to go back to the car and ask Murray to lend me some money. He said: "You must be joking. I've just given you £128,000."

I didn't know what I was going to do with the money. I wasn't going to do anything hastily and I just left it all where it was. I wasn't pressurised by Murray or Frank Greenwood — they knew it would take time for it to sink in. I wasn't in need of the vast amount of money so it might as well stay where it was, spread about in building societies. As soon as it became public knowledge, it was amazing how many people pestered me, especially insurance brokers, including one who suggested I should invest the entire money with his company and it would make a fortune in years to come. I left the money alone for a year, occasionally getting into a predicament by not remembering where it was. Before I left for Tasmania I asked Murray to check on figures I had been given by the brokers and see if there weren't people who had helped me who could come up with similar investments. I left signed cheques so that the money could go where they said and those two investments are the best I've ever made. I will reap the rewards in a few years' time, then Jack Simmons can think about retiring, even from cricket. I was not allowed to pay people for helping me but I was expected to buy something in recognition for their work. I had to make up my mind before I knew the amount raised and I bought them all a carriage clock so every time they looked at the time it would remind them. They were all presented at a committee dinner. I also bought something more for Murray because of his extra involvement and position as chairman. It wasn't extravagant. He'd always wanted a bat with a painting on it of Jack Simmons, so I got that and something else as well.

I came in for some criticism after the benefit, one source being a former Lancashire secretary, Jimmy James, then at Hampshire, who said a beneficiary was allowed to select the most popular and lucrative fixture as his benefit match, in my case the Roses match with Yorkshire. The suggestion was that I got the gate receipts which was big revenue being taken out of the county's pocket. But Lancashire beneficiaries have not taken gate receipts since 1967 and all I was allowed in the benefit was a collection on the first two days and a raffle on the third. Another secretary said benefits of the magnitude of mine competed with the clubs' money-raising schemes. Benefits could be stopped if cricketers were paid in proportion to other sports but we're not. And footballers, who earn vast amounts of money, still have benefit matches.

I had known that if the figure was high, I would have to consider how it would affect future beneficiaries and the chance of benefits being taxed. I spoke to Frank Greenwood and Murray about it and was told all the rules and regulations of the Inland Revenue and the Test and County Cricket Board had been strictly adhered to, that there was nothing at all to feel guilty about. Every function, every penny had been audited and the books were taken to the Inland Revenue before they asked for them. No fault could be found locally and they were sent to London and only six weeks after the presentation we received a letter from the Inspector of Taxes to say the benefit had been conducted in a correct and established way and only the interest that had accumulated should be taxed. I paid £1,000-plus of taxable income straight away. That letter came a week before the Players' Association meeting where it was even suggested I should have announced £78,000 instead of £128,000. I put that to Murray and Frank who said: "If we had done that, and why should we seeing it was made legitimately, where would we have put the other £50,000. Under the bed?" I would have had to spend it stupidly just to get rid of it. However, in the end, it is not just the money that counts, but the pure enjoyment I get from playing cricket and the friends I have made within the game.

13
IT'S BEEN A PLEASURE

One of the greatest pleasures of my years in first-class cricket has been to rub shoulders with the truly great players in the world. I have also enjoyed meeting the game's characters, helped some players hopefully to develop, and when the day does come when I have to retire from cricket I will have a mountain of memories. Here are just a few of the men I have played with and against since first getting into Lancashire's first team in 1968.

Farokh Engineer. Nobody loved the big occasion more than Farokh. If you thought you had seen the best of him he could raise his game again when the television cameras were at the ground. He enjoyed publicity and the glamour of being an Indian Test star and he took to the limelight like a duck to water. It became a joke at Old Trafford that whenever we had a photo taken you could guarantee that Farokh would always be in the centre, next to the trophy or the main person. When we did the double in 1970 we were invited to the Town Hall, all of us in black dinner jackets except Farokh who had a white one. He wasn't around when the photographs were being taken with the Mayor and we pressed the photographer to get the pictures before he arrived, but when they came out, sure enough, there was Farokh, right in the middle again, next to the Mayor.

Clive Lloyd, of course, had a big bearing on the side and its success in the early 1970s but it was Farokh who made the team so well balanced and helped us become a force. The runs he got at Test level didn't materialise all that often for Lancashire but his selection allowed us to pick five batsmen and five bowlers as well. He was a high-class wicket-keeper, his runs were a bonus and we've never been able to have the balance since he finished playing in 1976. He was so flexible, too. He could open the innings — and it is worth remembering that he scored a century by just after lunch on the opening day of a Test against the West Indies when Wes Hall and Charlie Griffith were playing — or go down the order. Wherever he played, he scored at breakneck pace. He could at times get the lads quite annoyed as he would be out to a stupid shot, yet he never slogged, as he didn't know how to. He simply played shots and could murder fast bowling, regardless of how quick the bowlers were, and feeding him bouncers was like giving cherries to pigs. I've always been an Alan Knott and Bob Taylor fan, but Farokh on top form was just as good a wicket-keeper. He was absolutely brilliant at times and I honestly cannot remember him dropping a catch.

Everybody connected with Old Trafford, and I think in particular the women, enjoyed his company. He said all the right things, was good to chat to, was pleasant and well-mannered, and a true gent in every way. He was great with children and was like the Pied Piper at grounds where the public could wander on the field. When he went out to practise he often went on his own, particularly at grounds like Liverpool, Southport and Blackpool, and he'd have the kids bowling to him and fielding and they loved it. I heard other counties' players say: "You can have our overseas player, he only wants to play when he fancies it." I don't think that ever applied to Farokh who liked success and enjoyed performing in front of his cricketing public. My disappointment was that he finished playing at least two years too early, and that was a major factor in Lancashire's decline. He was good in the dressing room, a Persian Indian, well mannered with a good education making a nice contrast with the likes of me from a working-class background and with Harry Pilling and John Sullivan who took the mickey and had some fun with him. True to type, though, Farokh always came through smiling to earn everybody's admiration as a person as well as a talented cricketer.

Colin Croft was such an unknown when he joined Lancashire that we thought we were getting one of the quickest left-handed bowlers in the world until we saw him bowling right-handed at the nets. He was signed for us immediately after taking 33 wickets against Pakistan in his first five Tests, and arrived a very raw youngster who had played only a handful of first-class games. I've never seen a rawer Test player. He couldn't field and we had to help him before games and on days off. He was so awkward, unlike the loose, gangling, athletic West Indians we had become accustomed to, and his bowling was unusual with a double whirl, a whirlwind action, coming up right behind the umpire and jumping out to bowl wide of the crease. The first time he played against Yorkshire, in 1977, I've never seen anybody bowl as fast. John Lyon, our wicket-keeper, took the first ball above his head and all of us in the slips moved back five yards. The next ball was quicker and we went back some more and I have never fielded as far back in the slips as I did to Croft that day. He beat everybody for sheer pace and we had them 64 for six in reply to our 270 for four when it rained and finished the match and again we thought: God's a Yorkshireman.

Croft worked at the airport in Georgetown in Guyana but wanted to become a pilot and would bring his books into the dressing room and instead of watching the game would start to study. Clive said to him once: "Every time we bat, Crofty, you have your head in a book. What are you doing?" Croft explained he wanted to become a pilot and was taking exams. It was around this time that he had been bowling badly where he couldn't control the direction or length of the ball which was going all over the place. Clive asked how long it would take him to qualify as a pilot and Croft said about four years. "Good," said Clive. "I'll have retired by then. There's no way I'll get in a plane with you the pilot. You don't know where the ball goes over a distance of twenty-two yards, how would you know where you're heading over thousands of miles?"

Croft was a loner, didn't drink or socialise much and when we were away from home he wanted to go in the first car back to the hotel, have a meal, usually Chinese or Indian and many times a takeaway, listen to music on record or tape, or watch television. Nobody minded that. What we did mind was when he started to decide when he wanted to bowl quick, when it wasn't always in the best interest of the side. Frank Hayes was captain at Worcester in 1978 and asked him to bowl to separate the last pair, Norman Gifford and Paul Pridgeon. But if he felt he shouldn't bowl, he wouldn't, and he ran up and bowled no quicker than Barry Wood. He just wouldn't bowl for the side and we didn't take that last wicket and finished up drawing the game. He did the same when I was captain at Southport and I told him to clear off to fine leg for the rest of the day. He wasn't retained after the 1978 season and knew he had been sacked before the Worcester game where he took three wickets in three balls. On the previous evening we had taken him with us to the pub, The Shakespeare, where he had had three bottles of Guinness and on the easiest of easy-paced wickets, he roared in the following morning. Ted Hemsley was the third "wicket," but it was a no ball. We thought heck, he's just been sacked and now we've found what makes him tick — three bottles of Guinness. Lancashire kept Croft's registration and he returned for one more season in 1982, this time under Clive Lloyd's captaincy. He seemed more sensible, more mature and gave Clive everything before getting a back injury.

Mick Malone was signed by Lancashire as their overseas player for 1980 after playing three matches in 1979 — and taking 19 wickets — and having a trial net with Neal Radford and Geoff Lawson. Unfortunately the conditions weren't good and they couldn't keep their feet too well as they performed in front of a handful of people including Cyril Washbrook, Brian Statham and Ken Grieves. Malone was good to have around, full of fun and pranks such as when he frightened Bob Ratcliffe by putting a rubber snake in his locker. Bob was terrified of snakes and when this one fell out of his locker he ran out of the dressing room and right out of the pavilion.

Mick played only one Test, just before Kerry Packer came on the scene, but was regarded as one of the best swing bowlers of the time. Outside his contract with the club he was being privately paid for the wickets he took and there were times he continued to play with injuries that made him less effective. But he always wanted to play, not for wickets and money though, I don't think he was that sort of a person. If he had taken a couple of games off when he was first injured we would have seen a better, more productive Malone, but the injuries got worse and he had to have quite a bit of time off at the end. In his contract Malone was to have a car, but it wasn't there when he arrived. He wasn't too disappointed because either David Lloyd or I would pick him up from his home in Haslingden and take him to Old Trafford, but he got fed up of waiting and said to me one evening: "Don't pick me up in the morning, Jack, I'll go in a taxi. Unless I do something drastic they won't do anything about it." So he went to Old Trafford and back in a taxi next day, got the bill and laid it on the secretary's desk. The car arrived soon after.

Michael Holding played only seven first-class matches for Lancashire, all in 1981 while he was professional with Rishton in the Lancashire League. One of the nicest people I've ever met, a truly great athlete who became a good friend due to our shared interest in backing horses. He didn't drink much, perhaps the occasional half of lager, or two, trained hard and was very fit and I wish he would have come full time to us. I never saw him annoyed at anything but he was so upset at a bad lbw decision against him early in the season that he cried. He thought he could win the game for us but was given out lbw to Ian Botham when he had hit the ball and we lost to Somerset by only 33 runs. Somebody said I should talk to him. We became good friends with the same tastes for food, and when he played for Tasmania at my suggestion our similar interests brought us together again: gambling, horses and casino.

He was a magnificent fast bowler and there was nothing more beautiful to watch in the game than Michael running up. When he first went off his short run I moved up a couple of yards at slip only for Clive Lloyd to pull me back. "He isn't any slower off his short run," he told me. "He just does it as a change." And our wicketkeeper took the next ball even higher than before. The fastest I ever saw Michael bowl was against England in Barbados in 1980–81 after West Indies had worked out a plan in which he would not use the opening over to warm up, and allow the batsman to face him at reduced pace. He went into the nets just before the start and really warmed up, then went off his long run for the most frightening over I've ever seen. And I was sitting in the stand. The ploy was not to give Geoff Boycott a sighting of the ball and it worked as he removed a stump or two. I said if I ever played against Michael I wanted one off the mark. Not two, just one, to take me to the other end. He promised me one in benefit matches, but said I hadn't a price in Test cricket. Which was all right seeing I'd never be chosen.

Barry Wood was one of the best players Lancashire have had in my years at the club, a terrific competitor who hated to lose, always tried to be a perfectionist and so followed the Geoff Boycott method of playing, he was more like Boycott than the man himself at times. He had to be an excellent player to get the number of gold medals he did although he had a far better chance than any other member of the side as he opened the batting and bowled as well. Some players thought he had an inflated opinion of his own ability but the confidence he had stood him in good stead. He was a fitness fanatic, everything he did was to make his game better and he was a great example to youngsters. He was sometimes accused of playing for himself a little bit too much although his anchor-man role allowed the later order batsmen to play shots. When he tried to accelerate himself he got out too many times — yet when you weigh everything up I'm sure he won more games for Lancashire than he lost.

He was a high-principled man and his opinion of his ability led him to believe he was worth more than the rest of the staff. He was thought of as a rebel, one who wanted more money, and when he got his £63,000 benefit in 1979 — a record at the time — he thought he had the upper hand and if he did not get more he would leave. All the senior and capped players were on the same wages at Lancashire, except Clive Lloyd as an overseas player, and I think this was a contentious issue for Barry, one I could never shift him on. I couldn't get over to him the difference in appeal to the public between him and Clive Lloyd. Wood did more than Clive in the team on occasions but it was a matter of trying to sell the game of cricket which was easier to promote when Clive was playing than if Barry Wood or Jack

Simmons were playing. He probably never came to terms with that and the contract with Lancashire was eventually withdrawn. Jack Bond had returned as manager at the start of 1980 and I'm sure he wouldn't have wanted Wood to leave but nor would he have a gun held at his head, so Wood left and joined Derbyshire.

Wood was a disciplinarian and a player who spent every hour he could in the nets, particularly batting, and he couldn't understand the more casual way I played the game, although I think he came to realise that that was the way I enjoyed doing it. But I liked his company, he talked a lot of sense and although he might disagree with you, he wouldn't ridicule your opinion. When he left Lancashire, almost as soon as he received his benefit cheque, it created a lot of bad feeling and discontentment among people who had helped him and when he left Derbyshire people reacted by accusing him of creating trouble there as well. He asked to come back to Lancashire and I for one would have taken him, for I felt somebody who knew him and who could possibly handle him could get the best out of a very good cricketer. Naturally, such decisions belong with committees and not players and the feeling of members, who were very irate about it, had to be considered. But as players always say — a benefit is for what you've done, not for what you are going to do, it is for your loyalty over the years you've been with a club. I'm just sorry to think that somebody who contributed so much to Lancashire cricket will probably only be remembered for leaving Lancashire after a record benefit. That's a sad thing.

Peter Lee came to Lancashire in 1972 on the recommendation of Jack Bond who thought he would be a good third seam bowler to Peter Lever and Ken Shuttleworth, to take over as stock bowler from Ken Higgs who had done the donkey work for many years, bowling into the wind. This is what he proved to be because he was a wholehearted player who hated to have the ball taken from him if there was something in the wicket. He had a good arm but he couldn't catch and on the few occasions when he caught one we thought we'd won the pools or reached a cup final. He never professed to be a batsman either but was one who always made you smile. He was nearly always the last man and after we'd asked him to support the other batsman we'd always watch him from the dressing room. Then he'd have a rush of blood and get out and every time he was out he never walked straight to the pavilion — he always went to the other batsman and apologised.

He was involved in a funny incident at Cardiff in one of his last games in 1981. It was Saturday night and we'd had a few drinks, eventually breaking up to leave "Leapy" with Clive Lloyd who was captain then. "Leapy" disappeared, never to return, leaving Clive to return to the hotel on his own and quite vexed. The following morning he tackled "Leapy" who had had a long bowl that day and after a few drinks had fallen asleep — in the toilets! When he wakened everywhere was in darkness, the place was closed and there was no way out. So he sat in a chair, fell asleep again and the next thing he heard was the sound of a vacuum cleaner. He frightened the cleaner to death when he showed himself and then walked out and returned to the hotel. But he had the last laugh. He got most wickets for us in the second innings and won the game for us.

Geoff Boycott said he rated Lee as highly as anybody in the country. He bowled a good line, was always doing something with the ball, digging it in at his ribs and Boycott felt he always had to be on his guard and top form to keep him out. That, I think, summed up "Leapy's" contribution to Lancashire cricket, eleven years in which he twice took over 100 wickets, the only Lancashire bowler to do that in the last seventeen years. The strain of bowling all the overs showed when he injured a muscle under his shoulder so badly that he had to have an operation which resulted in him having his arm in a sling for twelve weeks. He had few opportunities after that and I thought if anybody deserved a benefit he did. He and Frank Hayes were capped in the same year but it was Hayes who got the benefit in 1983 when Lee was released with a golden handshake. I suppose a severance payment is very nice and hasn't been done many times by Lancashire but I felt very disappointed for "Leapy" who had given such magnificent service and had missed a benefit of probably over £30,000.

Viv Richards. When Viv goes out to bat he doesn't walk, he swaggers, moving his hips and shoulders with an air of authority that is saying he is better than any bowler he is going to face. He did exactly the same in his debut which was against Lancashire at Taunton at the start of the 1974 season, the same game in which Ian Botham was also presented to the public. Viv came in, smacked four fours in two overs and we all looked on him as something of a slogger. Then we analysed it later and realised they weren't slogging, cross-bat shots, but genuine ones, through the covers, a cut, a pull and an on-drive. Maybe he wanted to impress, not only his teammates but the Lancashire side who were then one of the top teams in the country. In the view of many fine judges he is the best player in the world, entertaining to watch, even when you're bowling at him.

I was in Tasmania when Viv was on his first tour of Australia under Clive Lloyd's captaincy and hadn't done anything by December when the team came to the island for a one-day and a three-day game. He opened the batting for the first time and I don't know whether it was to try to cool him down, make him less free in his stroke play, but the idea proved a winner. He opened in Launceston in the one-day game and I got him out on 98 as he attempted to hit me over the stand. If he had got runs for the height of the ball he'd have been 106. He opened again at Hobart and started where he'd left off, batting carefully, picking the right balls to hit, getting into his rhythm and into touch for the Test. He reached his 100 and I thought he must be getting tired so I threw one up, hoping he would attempt to slog from the crease and hit straight in the air again. I was willing to try anything at the time. He didn't walk down the wicket, he ran down and hit it over the stand and the dressing rooms and into the river. Thankfully, they declared then.

Another innings of his I remember particularly well came during a Benson and Hedges match at Bath in the last year of David Lloyd's captaincy when, during the team talk before the game, Lloyd said he had a plan to combat Viv. He said I was our most accurate bowler and I would have to come on when Viv started playing shots. I thanked him very much. It was a compliment that the captain thought I might contain the great batsman. His plan was for me to bowl blockhole balls at leg stump which, hopefully, he would flick away. He would have six fielders on the legside, three in and our three quickest in the outfield and hope all he would get was a single. In he came, had a look at the bowling for about six balls, started to play a few shots and when I came on he was about 15. I put the plan into operation and it worked for about four overs which cost me four singles to Richards. Well done captain, I thought. Then Viv realised what was happening and before I could start another over he had a word with his partner, Brian Rose. That over he hit me for six twos, all carefully weighted shots followed by quick running. Six twos doesn't sound bad but it's not good in limited-over cricket and at the end of that over Lloyd came to me and said I had better turn to Plan B. I said we hadn't discussed Plan B and he said he knew, but I'd got the ball, I'd better think of one. So I bowled slightly outside off stump, a careful line with only three fielders on the offside, and he blocked the first ball. Had I by accident hit on Viv Richards' weakness? The second ball was pushed to mid-off and I thought, Heavens, he doesn't like it out there. The third went like a bullet to extra cover — no run — and the next ball he came down the wicket, leant back and hit it back over my head. I didn't need to watch where it was going, I knew it was a six. But behind me was a big civic building, about eighty feet high, and the ball hit the building near the top, bounced back and rolled to within three or four yards of my bowling mark. The next ball went for four and the last for a single and as he came down to my end, he smiled. David Lloyd asked me what I thought. I said: "Well, it's one run better than the last over." I said he'd tried Plan A, I'd used Plan B, I thought he ought to try Plan C. "We didn't discuss it. What is it?" he asked. I said: "For pity's sake take me off." And he did.

Every dog has his day and in 1983 I got him out three times, two of them in the championship match at Old Trafford after he had hit Les McFarlane, our West Indian seamer, for nine fours in three or four overs. Clive Lloyd was captain and suggested I bowled, which didn't thrill me at all, but in my opening over the ball turned and an inside edge gave David Lloyd the catch at leg slip. What a relief to get him out for 37. We took a lead of 170 on the first innings and in the second Viv, who wasn't feeling too well, batted lower down the order and came in to a turning wicket after I'd taken a couple of wickets. As he walked out I asked Clive if I could have a fielder close in at short leg, as well as one on the offside. He said: "Do you know who's coming in?" I said I did and felt we might as well put him under pressure. Clive said I could have a fielder if I could get somebody to stand there. Everybody had gathered round from the previous wicket and when I turned to see who would field there, they had all wandered off to their positions. "Surely somebody will stand there for a few balls," I said. The only person to answer was young Nasir Zaidi, our Pakistani leg spinner who called for his helmet. Before Richards had scored he turned a ball off bat and pad, and Zaidi dived to catch it. I was pleased as punch and I ran down the wicket to Zaidi who was running away on a lap of honour, chased by the other players. That is the amount of importance attached to getting the great man out. The only thing that bothered me was that perhaps he had a long memory and might get his revenge next time we met. It took two years for us to clash again, the end of the 1985 season, and who got the great man out, who took his wicket again, but the brilliant Simmons. "I. V. A. Richards c Fairbrother b Simmons . . . 120!" An innings including 11 fours and five sixes, a couple of them off me and landing in the seats behind. My analysis? 18-3-95-1. He had remembered!

Ray Illingworth. When Jack Bond was Lancashire's captain he always wanted us to watch the game we were playing in. There was always something to be learned, but during a game at Bournemouth in my early years with the club, Jack called me away from the dressing-room window where I was watching the lads bat against Hampshire. He had got hold of a television set and Ray Illingworth was bowling in the Test match, against India, I think it was. "Watch this man," he told me. "When he isn't bowling you can watch Lancashire bat. But while he is bowling watch him, his field placings and assess what he's trying to do." After that I became more and more an Illingworth fan and I hope I can now say he is a friend, and will be as long as we live. He must be one of the finest captains England have ever had and it speaks volumes for his leadership that we regained the Ashes under him in Australia in 1970–71. When he was captain everybody seemed to know what to do and he had the knack of getting the best out of players. When you think where Leicestershire were before Illingworth went there and what they achieved under him, it proves how good a player and captain he was. He's a great tactician, one of the best I've ever played against. I'm only sorry I never had the chance to play with him. But he was always willing to give me help with my bowling — one off spinner to another.

Ian Botham. His first game in county cricket was against Lancashire at Taunton at the start of the 1974 season, a youngster with a little pace as a bowler and a batsman who gave the impression that he was a slogger. He's always wanted to hit the ball really hard and he has always been confident, even as a youngster. It might have looked like big-headedness but to me it was just confidence in his own ability and where he was heading. His innings at Leeds in 1981 and his bowling in the next Test, at Birmingham, has to put him as the most dynamic and best all-rounder there has ever been. Nobody empties bars the way he does, and nobody is bored when he is around.

During England's tour of Australia in 1978–79 I went to Launceston airport to meet Mike Hendrick, Bob Willis, Bob Taylor and Botham who had all arrived before the others. I got on particularly well with Hendrick so I took him and Botham in my car, a Tasmania committee man took the other two. I wanted to pick something up from the flat on the way and Botham asked me if it was possible to stay at our house for a while, watch television, and have a home-cooked meal. He was looking to get away from the everyday grind of hotel life, to relax in somebody's home. He wasn't drinking at the time, and while Hendrick and I had beer, Botham was happy to have a cup of tea, eat the mixed grill and chicken, sit in an arm chair and watch television.

In recent years I have become a director of Burnley Football Club and during Somerset's visit to Old Trafford at the end of the 1985 summer I took him, Colin Dredge, Trevor Gard and

Allan Border's brother John to watch a football match at Burnley. I don't know how good Botham is at soccer but I do know he has a great love for it and is a great competitor who would give 150 per cent to anything he did. He said cricket had given him a good life but his first love in sport had always been soccer.

Mike Brearley is a player who will be remembered, I suppose, for his captaincy of England and Middlesex rather than his batting, which had limitations. In the early stages he was a restricted player, one you could control to a point. He was good on the onside, steady, not classical, not easy to get out, more a man-made than a natural player. He knew exactly what his strengths were, played within his limitations and didn't try to emulate anybody. As a captain he seemed able to handle most players, was a great thinker of the game, one who was full of new ideas. The first time I saw him in a one-day game, before four players had to stay within the circle, he even put the wicketkeeper half or three quarters way to the boundary to stop the thin edge. He was a successful Middlesex captain with a successful side and perhaps his one failure was Phil Edmonds who openly didn't get on with him, dropped out of the England team and has only returned under Mike Gatting at Middlesex and David Gower at England level. I once invited Brearley and Middlesex teammates Graham Barlow and Clive Radley for dinner and when we were talking about cricket I noticed how Barlow and Radley reacted to him, a respect and acceptance of a nice person and good cricket brain. When he gave up the captaincy of England and Middlesex, both sides didn't do quite so well to start with. When he returned to captain England he again showed his ability to get the best out of every player and make each one feel a necessary part of a good side that is capable of winning. His captaincy of the England side on tour was outstanding and I know he got criticism in Australia for not getting runs, but he maintained that a captain as a batsman was still an all-rounder, like Jack Bond.

In 1980 I was invited to go to India and one of the main reasons I went was to assess him first-hand and play under him instead of always against him. He was impressive, did everything I expected, was jovial or strict at the right time, would go out with the lads some times, stay away on other occasions. On that trip I bought eight leather handbags for Jacqueline and my mother and he always says now: "Have you got rid of all those handbags yet?"

I thought Brearley was wrong in his book on captaincy to criticise Clive Lloyd and say Lancashire had won nothing under him. Clive took a young side to three semi-finals, Brearley often played with nine Test players in his side, which must be a great advantage. I have a great regard for Brearley as a person and captain but if you can't captain a side with the talent and balance of Middlesex you can't captain anybody. At least that was his argument about Clive's captaincy of West Indies with their talent. But you still have to look after the players and nine or ten super stars can be very temperamental and jealous. Maintaining team spirit, getting everybody to play for the side is an important factor for a captain. That is why Clive Lloyd has done well — and Mike Brearley, too.

David Boon. When I first went to Tasmania in 1972 I saw this youngster — he was then barely twelve — in a none too wealthy school, Charles Street, which didn't have too many facilities. It couldn't be classed as a very good area of Launceston and with its shortage of facilities youngsters had to go to East Launceston School for coaching. I had ten or twelve boys from each school and when I spoke to Boon I learned he was a reasonable swimmer and quite a good footballer. As a cricketer I had never seen a boy who could play as straight and seemed to have the time to play shots. I told his parents I thought he was something special and his father said: "If you think so, I'll make sure he's there whenever you want him." I gave the best boys more advanced coaching and he improved no end: at the age of twelve he scored a century in an under-13 side on the Launceston ground. He was only tiny, but stocky, and his progression continued though he was always playing against older boys.

Boon was my blue-eyed boy and I treated him like a son. His approach tactically and mentally was good, he wanted to learn and was at the nets at every opportunity. He toured England with an Australian under-19 side, got into the Tasmanian squad while still only seventeen and became a Test player at twenty-three. There was a chance of David going to South Australia but several influential people in Tasmania got together to organise a package deal, supported by sponsorship, to hold on to perhaps the best player Tasmania have ever seen come up through the ranks. Greg Ritchie outshone David in England in 1985 but I still think Boon is the superior player. But then I'm biased and have been for years. Happily, there is room for them both in the Australian team.

Dennis Lillee. Here is a man who has had more brushes with the establishment than any other Australian player, who was a fiery, aggressive fast bowler, yet off the field was one of the quietest of men who didn't like to be the centre of attraction. During England's tour of Australia in 1978–79 I went out with Mike Hendrick and Chris Old, and Lillee joined us for drinks and a meal and for a presentation not far out of Melbourne where he shunned the limelight and sat on a bar stool in the kitchen and chatted to anybody who came to him. A great thrill came for me when I was commentating for the ABC in Devonport during Tasmania's match against Western Australia and he had to leave the field injured, unable to play any further part in the game. He spent the whole session chatting to me and when kids — loads of them — came for his autograph, he said, very quietly: "I'll sign all your autographs, lads. I'm just talking to a friend at the moment." They all got his signature and one woman, who already had his autograph, asked if he would get Kim Hughes's for her. He took her book and told her to be at the dressing room five minutes after the finish. Whatever differences existed between Lillee and Hughes weren't evident to me when he took me in the dressing room and, after introducing me, said: "Skipper, will you sign this for me, please?" which Hughes did. When Lillee went to the door with the book, Rod Marsh told me he never refused kids an autograph. "If there's anything wrong with him, he signs too many," he said. Still, I'm sure it makes a youngster happy when such a great player, a great hero, signs for you. I thought Lillee a fine man.

Ian and Greg Chappell. Two great cricketers, but in different ways. Ian a good leader of men, aggressive and gritty; Greg more gentlemanly, perhaps more aloof and a technically better batsman than Ian.

Ian was a very courageous batsman, more of a backfoot player to quick bowlers and very hard to get out. He was a fine captain, the sort who went out on a limb for his players, a great team man who wouldn't ask anyone to do anything he wouldn't. He was typically Australian in that he didn't deliberately cheat but left it all to the umpires and would even defend his own players against umpires to the extent of taking on the establishment. I admired him greatly. I played against him in a benefit match at Lytham when he went in first on a poor wicket, played competitively, grafted and worked hard for 40 odd before he was one of the last out. It thrilled me to see him in a so-called benefit match willing to risk being hurt. He came to congratulate me when we won but I could see he was annoyed, he so hated to lose. He built that into his Australian side and while he had a great attack with bowlers such as Lillee and Thomson and Walker, he moulded them into a team. Unfortunately he might be remembered more for his aggressive attitude than all the good things he did, particularly for his players.

Greg was the best on-driver I've ever seen. If he had a weakness, and this is purely from hearsay, it was against out and out quick bowlers on bouncier wickets, a consideration that never entered into it with Ian. I played against Greg when he was with Queensland and he always appeared nice and never used aggravation or verbal abuse on the field, which Ian did.

14
BACK AT LORD'S

Jack Bond's retirement as captain after the 1972 season marked a turning point in Lancashire's fortunes. We had won the John Player League twice and the Gillette Cup three times in his last four years as captain. In the next four years we were to reach the Gillette Cup final three times more, but only once as winners. Then we had to go eight years before we had any success again, winning the Benson and Hedges Cup by beating Warwickshire at Lord's in 1984. Maybe we would have started to slip even if Bond had stayed on as captain for a year or two longer. Who knows? But all captains have their own ideas, their own thoughts about players and tactics and how to run a side and a team's performances are often a true reflection of the influence a captain has had on the other players.

David Lloyd was the man chosen to succeed Bond and everybody knew he was being groomed for the job. There were occasions, the players would say, that if Bond went to the bathroom, Lloyd was there as well. He set his stall out to get the captaincy and convinced Bond that he had the right qualities to do it. I am sure he had — on the field, but not off it where he was far too immature. He was a good county player, later to become a Test player, quite a jovial person and now one of the best after-dinner speakers there is. But in those earlier years he was a person who couldn't really control himself. If he got out in the closing stages of the day, especially if he'd had to bat the last half-hour, he was quite likely to hit the wall of the dressing room with his bat. He was quite mad as a car driver, and you could tell if he was annoyed or upset by the way he drove as he went at eighty miles an hour on country roads, frightening many players, then sixty on the motorway. He was due to drive home from Ilford once after a bat-throwing episode and I asked if I should drive. He could sleep in a car so he agreed. I said to him: "You know you're being groomed to captain Lancashire and I believe you'll get it. But if you show rushes of temper, more or less indicating you can't handle yourself, I doubt very much if you'd get the job if word of it got back to the committee." He was very concerned about that and controlled himself more after that and became a better person.

When he became captain, there were players who weren't keen on him having it, partly because he was only twenty-six years old, and there were doubts over whether he could handle himself. But team spirit was so good everybody just wanted to play for Lancashire, regardless of who was captain. Whoever followed Bond was going to have a hard job but I think I would have gone for Peter Lever as somebody who could get the best out of players and who was even-tempered in his dealings with players. But he was also regarded as a rebel, the Arthur Scargill of Lancashire, and I'm sure that went against him when Bond's successor was considered. Clive Lloyd, too, could have become captain and I think Harry Pilling would have done a reasonable job. David Lloyd could then have taken over the captaincy two or three years later and if that had happened I believe he would still be playing and would have had an excellent chance of captaining England. During Lancashire's problems with players' salaries in 1975 he didn't seem prepared to do anything about it when he should have shown more leadership and taken the problems of a number of players to the committee and insist they be quickly sorted out.

On the field I regarded him as one of the best tacticians I've ever played under and I think he had ambitions of going on to captain England. He was highly regarded as a player but I think the Test selectors made a mistake in taking him to Australia after sending Barry Wood to India. It was the wrong way round. Lloyd was a fine player of spin bowling, Wood responded to quick bowling though I think Lloyd did extremely well against the might of Lillee and Thomson at their peak on the 1974–75 tour. Lloyd took a battering in Australia but still averaged quite high and stood up to it better than Keith Fletcher or Dennis Amiss. I also felt that when you are attacked by high-class fast bowling match after match you get slightly shell-shocked and you don't want to face any more. Lloyd came home with a neck injury, didn't play Test cricket again, although he did get into the one-day side, and had had enough of captaincy by the end of the 1977 season. That was one of the worst in Lancashire's history, next to the bottom of the John Player League and championship, knocked out of the Gillette Cup in the second round and failed to qualify for the knockout stages of the Benson and Hedges Cup for the first time.

Frank Hayes took over as captain in 1978 and was probably in a more commanding position as captain than either Bond or Lloyd, having been given sole power of team selection which I've always thought better than a selection committee. On occasions I was brought in for discussion on the side with our coach, John Savage, but Hayes, of course, always had the last word. He was good at handling people but didn't like hassle or argument and much preferred a quiet life. He took over when Lancashire were at a low ebb and during his three years as captain we achieved little as we continued in the bottom half of the championship and made hardly any challenge for any of the one-day competitions. We had slipped back to the 1960s and from being a formidable side capable of beating anybody under Bond we had become an ordinary team of few attractions.

Jack Bond returned to Lancashire in 1980 as team manager, a move that was welcomed by everybody and which we all thought would bring about the change in fortunes we so badly needed. He had been away for six years after becoming captain of Nottinghamshire in 1974 and then moving to the Isle of Man where he was coach and groundsman of the King William School. Jack, of course, had been my first captain at Lancashire and I can remember my first impression was of a fatherly figure, older than anybody else in the side, looked up to and respected. He was the last captain we have had who would fight for his players, irrespective of whether he was totally in agreement with them, and he would always try to sort out any grievances. He was the most unselfish of men, always thinking about everybody else ahead of himself. If the wicket was good he would let players like Frank Hayes, David Hughes, Ken Snellgrove, John Sullivan or myself go in to bat before him. If the wicket or the bowling was more difficult he would go in and take the responsibility, something he was always prepared to do, and was a batsman who excelled when the pressure was on and the side were doing badly. When runs were needed Bond was your man.

When the John Player League started in 1969 he didn't take the attitude of some that this wasn't a game of cricket. He always took the attitude that if a game of cricket was there to be played then you played it as well as you could and he instilled into us that fielding was the biggest asset to any side in restricted overs. If anybody came off that field without grass stains on their flannels he wanted to know why. In those early days there weren't too many players who had the ability or even thought of playing anything other than the normal, traditional shots, the ones in the coaching manual. Then batsmen started to improvise and adapted to the requirements of the game. Jack showed faith in his spinners and encouraged batsmen like Barry Wood and John Sullivan to develop their bowling as well. As a captain, and not just in one-day matches, he thought everybody in the side had to play for Lancashire County Cricket Club, that it had to be a team effort in every respect. He would ask batsmen to commit suicide, to go out and blast runs, and that is why he never used averages to make up his mind on team selection. He had to report back to the committee but never let them have averages and when choosing middle-order players he always took into consideration what he had asked that player to do.

He was a very astute tactician who got the best out of players, encouraging some, criticising others. He used psychology, certainly with me, for when I would get annoyed at not being put on to bowl he would say he had saved me — and on many occasions it worked. There was a great enjoyment off the field with the team always together, talking a lot about cricket. We were bound together then, just like one person. Before the start of one game at Old Trafford we were having a team meeting when the secretary came in and said there would be a win bonus for the side. Jack told him to clear off as we were having a tactics talk and money wasn't going to make us play any harder or better. I thought the money would come anyway but though we won the match we didn't receive it. Whether the secretary at that time thought he'd been treated harshly in being told to get out of the dressing room, I don't know. But Jack never bothered about money. He just wanted to enjoy his life and make sure the family were all right. It showed the person he was during his benefit year in 1970, the year after we won the John Player League for the first time, the season we won it again along with the Gillette Cup and were the best and most exciting one-day team in England. He received £7,400 which was a disgrace, but he seemed pleased at the effort put in by various committees and was grateful. To have received only that amount of money was poor reward for somebody who had revitalised Lancashire cricket, but he accepted it with good grace and I think he had spent it all within eighteen months on a new kitchen for his wife, Florence, a car and a good holiday.

All in all he was the best captain I have played under. I have enjoyed playing under Clive Lloyd but I played under Jack a bit longer and first impressions are lasting impressions and watching him and learning from him helped me become a successful captain in Tasmania. He is a highly generous man and Jacqueline and myself have become good friends with the Bonds through the years, a friendship I felt stopped my progression, first in having to wait as long as I did to get my county cap, and maybe not getting the chance to captain Lancashire. I didn't feel I was ready in 1972 when he made it clear that David Lloyd was being groomed to succeed him and when he gave it to John Abrahams in 1984 I thought then I'd been passed over.

I think his regard for Lancashire youth cricket and wanting the up-and-coming players to be Lancashire born and bred is admirable but I feel there have been times when players from overseas and other counties would have strengthened our team. I feel the emphasis on home-grown players has stopped our progress and denied us the chance of winning more. I know how difficult it is when you're the person making the decisions and it is easy for me to say this without being in the position of having to decide, but I think success, even if it is with the help of outside players, within reason, is better for Lancashire, its members, supporters and players. But Jack Bond has always been the Boss to me, whether as captain or manager, always a likeable person and easy to talk to. The four of us once took a motoring holiday through France to Benidorm and on a few occasions he was still bossing me: Come on, Simmo, get this done or get that done, or "Have you got the kettle on?" And I'd turn round and say: "Hey, you're not bloody captain here." And he'd just laugh. We've had some great times.

Clive Lloyd became captain of Lancashire in 1981 after Frank Hayes had held the position for three years and during Jack Bond's second year as manager. I have always held the highest regard for Clive and today we are in business together. The first time I met him, though I had seen him on television in Cavalier games, was when he was professional with Haslingden in the Lancashire League in 1968, a powerful hitter, a marvellous fielder and clearly many great years ahead of him. He was qualifying for Lancashire that year and I was asked to pick him up at Haslingden for what was to be my first second XI game since 1961. He was quietly spoken without any brashness whatsoever and we hit it off straightaway. He played quite a few second-team matches that year and one first-team game, against the Australians.

Clive has always been able to accept criticism or a bit of fun about colour, providing it is meant in a light-hearted way and will tell jokes about himself. I've never had any qualms about telling a joke about a coloured person because Clive would be the first to laugh. He is anti-apartheid, as you might expect, and was brought up to believe that no matter what your colour you should not be a second-class citizen. He has told me of offers he has had to go to South Africa and I could hardly believe them. He was once offered a million dollars for two or three six-week tours and you have to be a high-principled person to turn that sort of money down. I don't know whether I could have done it.

I went to the West Indies in 1972–73 when England were playing there and Frank Hayes was a member of their team. I've never wanted to push myself on Lancashire teammates in Test cricket, but Clive took me into the West Indies dressing room to watch from their viewing area. I've always got on with West Indies players, I feel at ease with them and regard many of the present team as my friends; until they bowl at me! I was in Australia during the 1981–82 season and during one visit to the West Indies dressing room at Melbourne, just for something to say, I asked some of the players what it was like to have the best player in the world on your side. They asked me who was the best player in the world and I said: "Viv Richards." They agreed he was a great player but said he wasn't the best in the world. I asked who was and they said: "The captain," meaning Clive, who was stretched out sleeping at the time. He always gets runs when they're needed, they said. He had a fantastic season that year and they chaired him off at Adelaide. So the man not only held respect as player and captain, but was regarded by his own team as the best batsman in the world.

I've had the privilege to see some great innings from Clive, a player for the occasion, one who has won cup semi-finals and finals for us. He's a very courageous player, too. I can still see his Gillette Cup innings against Surrey in 1977, shortly before he had cartilage operations when his knees were giving him real trouble. He looked ready for the grave in that match and was so bad that he couldn't go up and down the steps properly but had to take them one at a time like a ninety-year-old. To go out and play the innings he did, of 86, was out of this world. He felt better when he came in at lunch time but he stiffened up again in the forty minute break, was more restricted afterwards and was bowled almost as soon as he got out again before he could get moving. He hit six sixes that day and though we lost he at least won the Man of the Match award. He played a wonderful innings of 126 in the 1972 Gillette Cup final against Warwickshire after we'd been 26 for two but the most powerful innings I've ever seen — and it surpassed even the one by Viv Richards at Old Trafford for West Indies against England in the one-day match in 1984 — came in the John Player League against Middlesex in 1981. We needed 219 to win and were 68 for two when Clive went in. That had become 87 for five when I got to the wicket with 132 wanted off not much more than 17 overs. "We can win this," he said. I thought he was crackers but never having been one to give up I said: "Right, I'll get the 32, you can get the 100." And he did. There was no restriction then of fielders in the circle and Mike Brearley had them all on the edge but was still powerless to halt Clive who was hitting the ball where he wanted. Wayne Daniel bowled with a long off and long on but Clive hit a straight six, low and flat and one of the most powerful shots I've ever seen. All I had to do when I had the strike was give it back to Clive and in a stand of 94 I scored just 24. Clive finished with 105 not out and hit the last ball for four for victory.

Clive has always been a team man. If quick runs were needed he never bothered about his image or his average going down the drain, he did what he was asked. I find it amazing just how much he does love Lancashire and the County Cricket Club and he now regards Lancashire as his home, not Guyana. His unselfishness, his desire to put the team first at all times, has cost him, I believe, between 30 and 40 hundreds in the seventeen years he has been with the county. His image as a cricket ambassador is second to none. I don't care who anybody names from the past or who might come in the future, I don't think anybody will have the same charisma as Clive. He is an easy going man, but he was upset recently by Mike Brearley's book on captaincy in which it was suggested that Clive had done nothing with Lancashire. Brearley's views on his leadership of West Indies didn't bother him because when you have his record you can take anything anyone tries to throw at you. Records show there has never been such a successful Test captain. But Brearley was unfair in his reference to Clive's captaincy of Lancashire who got to three Cup semi-finals in his first three-year spell and with a bit of luck would have got into two finals. Clive was hurt and I feel that if he'd had a little more time he would have brought the best out of a young, inexperienced side.

It was during Clive's term of office that I had one of my biggest disappointments during my years with Lancashire. In 1982 I topped the batting and bowling averages in championship matches and in all cricket took 72 wickets and scored over 700 runs. Yet I was offered only a one-year contract while players who hadn't done as well were given two years. That made me as annoyed as I've ever been because I felt it was an insult to the performances I'd had that season. It appeared to me that they didn't want me to continue and I thought about going into league cricket. I asked the manager, Jack Bond, why I had been offered only a one-year contract. He said it was purely because of my age. I don't think till then I'd ever thought of my age. I would be forty-two through the 1983 season which, presumably, they thought I could get through, but if I had a bad year, surely nobody would believe that I'd simply turn up at Old Trafford the following season purely for the money. If I had broken down at any time I wouldn't have wanted to let myself, the club or the other players down. I wouldn't have needed telling if I had to retire; if I felt it was time to finish I wouldn't have held Lancashire to the contract. Our chairman, Cedric Rhoades, gave me exactly the same reason and, knowing how disappointed I was, he said if I wanted a contract at the end of the 1983 season I would get one. I said that wasn't the point. Others, who hadn't done as well as me, had got two years and there didn't appear to be a future for me, other than year by year. The chairman said he would bring the matter up at the next committee meeting.

Even so, I came closer than I've ever been to not re-signing and after I had spoken to the captain and chairman of Fleetwood, the Northern League side, in a Preston pub, I definitely decided then to leave Lancashire. I never talked money with Fleetwood but I would have gone for £4,000 which, by today's standards, isn't high. We met later in an hotel in Manchester when I was told they didn't think they could afford me, that they were going back to a cheaper professional, about £1,500 or £2,000. "And you wouldn't sign for that," they said. I asked if they were sure and was then told there were other reasons: if they signed me perhaps they wouldn't get a benefit match or a Lancashire second team game which they enjoyed having. I didn't pursue it. The "offer" was withdrawn and I thought heck, if you can't beat them, join them, so I swallowed my pride and went to the Lancashire secretary's office and signed the one-year contract. Within days I left for Tasmania and soon after arriving a letter arrived offering me a two-year contract. I can't say how delighted I was. I hadn't really wanted to go to a club.

I had second thoughts early in the 1983 season because I felt tired after coming back from Tasmania. I thought I had put myself under a lot more pressure and I desperately didn't want to let Lancashire down after their renewed faith in me. But I proved my fitness, had my best-ever all-round season which made me one of *Wisden*'s Cricketers of the Year, a great thrill for me. When I had been offered a one-year contract at the end of 1982 I had told the players of my disappointment and cleaned out my locker. I told them all I didn't expect to see them the following year and hoped they had a good season. When I returned at the start of 1983 they had opened my locker and written inside: "Good to see you back, Simmo. We knew you couldn't leave." I think Graeme Fowler was responsible and I appreciated it very much. I was sure I was going to last those two years, even if I went out there on crutches.

The results were there over those two years and I was relieved. For at the start of the 1984 season I bowled 47 overs in the match against Derbyshire, a lot in the first game, and injured my back. I was in too much pain to play in the first Benson and Hedges match but a week off enabled me to recover properly and help Lancashire get into the quarter finals of the competition where we were drawn to play Essex, the favourites. The game was at Chelmsford, one of the hardest fixtures we could have had, yet I had the feeling, from fully a week before, that we could win. We bowled them out cheaply and won quite easily and David Hughes and myself went in the bar afterwards and must have had four large gin and tonics each. I was dancing and rock and rolling on the coach going home after taking one for 25 in my 11 overs and then hitting the winning run that gave us a four-wicket win. We then went to Nottingham to the new favourites and had an amazing win after Alan Ormrod, our opening batsman, had been declared unfit and Mark Chadwick, only twenty-one years old, had been brought in. I was not so confident here but we had the run of the ball, Graeme Fowler was dropped early in his innings and Chadwick, in his first Benson's match, won the game for us and was Man of the Match. We were back at Lord's and I desperately wanted to win my first final there for eight years and with a completely different side apart from David Hughes, John Abrahams and me. I had a marvellous bowling spell, we fielded superbly and that, next to the Gillette Cup final win with Tasmania, was my greatest thrill in cricket, not so much for the match itself but for coming back with another side and winning again. I always said if I won another medal I'd retire, but who could think of retiring at such a time? I was pleased for everybody, perhaps more for Abrahams in his first year as captain only two years after being capped.

Lancashire were also near the top of the John Player League at the time after winning six of our first nine games, and the day after the Lord's match we travelled to Taunton to play Somerset. They were without Viv Richards and Joel Garner, as we were without Clive Lloyd because of the West Indies tour, but there was still Ian Botham to reckon with. They got 208 for eight, a reasonable score, but what pleased me was the attitude of our players. It was a very hot day and I thought the effort and draining of energies from Lord's mentally and physically, would have had a bearing on our performance, but we fielded where we had left off at Lord's and we won easily after an innings of 91 from Steve O'Shaughnessy who was so exhausted he had to drag his bat from the wicket to the pavilion when he was out.

The only disappointment of that final run in was our game against Warwickshire at Old Trafford when we still had a chance of the title. In all previous games I had been asked to look at the wicket and give my opinion on whether we should bat or field first. The wicket wasn't looking that good, they were out of the running for the title, and as they were a good run-chasing side with such players as Dennis Amiss, Alvin Kallicharran and Geoff Humpage, I felt we should put them in if we won the toss. When I discovered that we had chosen to bat first — and I hadn't been asked my opinion — I just couldn't believe a decision like that had been made after the way we'd been playing. We had curbed all sides by the brilliance of our fielding and had won seven out of nine games batting second that summer. I was vice-captain of the side but I hadn't been consulted and I was seething at what I considered was a snub. If Clive Lloyd, the greatest captain in Test history, can ask other people's opinions, anybody can. It doesn't matter whether the captain takes any notice, just as long as he makes people feel part of the running of the team. John Abrahams said the wicket was so bad it would disintegrate quickly and would be worse for the side batting second. That was something I had never seen in sixteen years of John Player cricket. It was not a good thing to say with our opening batsmen, Graeme Fowler and O'Shaughnessy, waiting to go in and I think we went out fearing the worst and thinking if we got to 150 we had a chance of winning. We reached 157 for seven and while they, too, lost seven wickets and won only in the 39th over, to me that proved my point. If the roles had been reversed, and we were on a high at the time, I don't think their bowlers would have had the will to stop us winning. I was annoyed throughout the match and I don't think it brought the best out of me. After the game I again tried to find out who had made the decision, but our manager, Jack Bond, said I must back my captain. Of course I did, but not to ask the vice-captain on such a vital issue after asking him in every other game seemed strange to me. My mind went back ten days when we had lost by an innings to Northamptonshire in the championship game at Southport after putting them in to bat. John Abrahams was then tackled in front of the pavilion by a committee man who pointed out "A Lancashire side never puts the opposition in." I can't help wondering if that had anything to do with the Warwickshire decision, which I felt had the biggest bearing that season on our position in the John Player League. That decision was so wrong it was ludicrous.

It was something of a surprise to most players when John Abrahams was given the captaincy in 1984 but I know Jack Bond felt he could be a good captain for the future. I must admit when Jack discussed it with me I was disappointed I hadn't been in his thoughts, even though I know that when you've turned forty you can only be a short-term appointment. But I've been passed over before and maybe it wasn't as big a disappointment this time. Abrahams' example in the field came through to us all, his batting improved and although I was upset towards the end of the John Player League season I still thought we had had quite a successful year by winning the Benson and Hedges, finishing fourth in the John Player and reaching the quarter-final of the NatWest Trophy. John's batting declined in 1985 and with it his confidence, so that he was putting himself down the order at times and giving the feeling of not being totally in charge. He was affected by his own batting performances and if he hadn't been captain, he would probably have been dropped. There were a few grumbles through the dressing room and it was no surprise when Lancashire didn't keep him as captain after 1985 but reappointed Clive Lloyd instead. John, I think would have benefitted by asking for more help. I know I felt blocked out even though I was vice-captain, that really my opinion wasn't wanted.

I know John Abrahams was disappointed, as I was, that we didn't sign Trevor Jesty when he left Hampshire. He would have strengthened the middle order and we would have been capable of out-batting most sides. The folly in not signing Jesty was emphasised when so many of our batsmen had a poor season in 1985. I know Jack Bond felt we should be encouraging home-grown players but in our great days in the early 1970s we had four or five players not born in Lancashire, yet in 1985 we usually only had three. So what was wrong with another outside player to stabilise the team and help bring on young players.

One of the wonderful things about cricket is the new experiences it can bring into your life . . . even after seventeen years. At the end of the 1985 season a team composed of Lancashire players, but under the banner of a Clive Lloyd XI, went to New York for six days where we played one limited-over match. The promoter, Bert Smith, hailed from the West Indies and Clive was the big drawing card for the largely Caribbean public that came to see a match in which we played the American All Stars, again mostly from the West Indies. The trip didn't get off to a good start when we had to wait at the airport in New York after a large metal container holding our bags slipped off the truck and crushed a man to death. There were a few hitches at the start when we had to change hotels, there was a cash-flow problem and two of our players, Graeme Fowler and Paul Allott, became disillusioned and went home.

They were unlucky because things settled down then and we all had a wonderful time as we were richly entertained and looked after by the Consul General Mr Kennedy and his assistant Mike Marshall. There was no cricket field where money could be taken so we played on a football ground. An area was rolled and matting was laid but conditions were dangerous and one or two players were hit including Clive who had gone out in front of 3,500 people to a hero's welcome and had been hit on the forehead and floored by one delivery. We had to put ice on his head, a lump came up and he was scarred but determined to bat on and not let people down and scored over 30. Chris Maynard was hit on the head while keeping wicket and David Varey took over behind the stumps and wore a helmet! Roger Harper, the West Indies off spinner, made up our team and helped us win comfortably. Some of the money we were owed arrived at half time from the gate receipts when Bert Smith, escorted by security men, came into the dressing room with a carrier bag containing 7,000 dollars in fives, tens and twenties. We enjoyed Manhattan and New York, made money and were treated well and two of the sponsors, Earl and Joy Levi, took us to a ball game where 40,000 people were watching the Mets. A top edge in baseball is a foul hit and one of the early ones flew into the stand where we were sitting. It would have hit Earl but I stood up and caught it one-handed. I was about to throw it back and I was told no, you have to keep it as a memento. The people round about me shouted in excitement, I was made to take a bow, presented with a pint of beer and a flag of the Mets. The hosts were thrilled to bits that they were with somebody who had caught the ball which I kept and brought home.

Although I have never been officially appointed captain of Lancashire, I have been vice-captain for many years and have led the team from time to time in championship and one-day matches. When Lancashire decided at the end of the 1985 season not to reappoint John Abrahams but to turn again to Clive Lloyd, I couldn't have been more delighted to have continued under his captaincy. That is not meant as any disrespect to the other Lancashire skippers I have been vice-captain to, but I'm sure that they, like me, recognise that here we have one of modern cricket's most outstanding leaders. If anybody can get the best out of a team, I believe Clive can and I regard it as an honour to be number two to him.

Clive Lloyd stands for all that is best in cricket and is a good example to all the young players coming through at Lancashire. He still has plenty to offer the game and the county and I feel sure we can benefit under his leadership. I knew when I was made vice-captain to him that I'd be expected to lead the side quite a few times in 1986 for the old Clive Lloyd legs aren't what they used to be and, of course, we have to play our other overseas player, Patrick Patterson, when the situation demands. That suits me fine for I feel the responsibility can do nothing but good for my game and I'll enjoy the challenge of helping to bring on youngsters who can be Lancashire's backbone for many years when we're gone. I just hope I can carry on without letting the side or myself down.

INDEX